GWR
JUNCTION STATIONS

GWR
JUNCTION STATIONS

Adrian Vaughan

LONDON
IAN ALLAN LTD

Published by Ian Allan Ltd,
Shepperton, Surrey; and printed by
Ian Allan Printing Ltd at their works
at Coombelands in Runnymede,
England

Contents

Illustrations from the Locomotive & General Railway
Photographs (L&GRP) Collection are reproduced
courtesy of David & Charles Ltd.

Introduction

Junction stations were sometimes planned as such — and sometimes not. Indeed, the general lack of planning even in some that were 'planned' is remarkable. They and the railway system generally were the product of a completely free enterprise system which brought idiosyncracies to the fore — all that was required was an Act of Parliament. Later on other Acts, like the 'Regulation of Railways' Act and bodies like the Railway Inspectorate of the Board of Trade were introduced to bring some order to the chaos. Safety did, and still does, cost a lot of money which, according to the minds of the railway pioneers, would be better spent on dividends. Public opinion inside and outside Parliament, the Railway Inspectorate and a certain maturity of outlook which can only develop with the passing years altered the corporate mind of the railway companies as it did in the other parts of the nation — everyone became a little bit more careful — but the old junction stations with their often eccentric layout and difficult operating procedures remained as a legacy of former days — a delight to the connoisseur, an expense to the company and a memorial to the *laisser faire* days of railway building.

Castle Cary was in existence for 50 years before it became a junction, a clean, straightforward fork built where it was not, because of the existence of Castle Cary station but because the GWR was building a new route to the West and Castle Cary was the furthest west that the existing line went before it turned sharply south for Weymouth. Until the 1980s the station was completely ignored by the West of England expresses that passed through, but continued to be served by its traditional trains. A few miles down the Weymouth line, Yeovil was a mass of junctions, each one added piecemeal with never a thought of tomorrow or of convenience. Honeybourne began as a wayside halt, shortly became a junction with the usual cramped, inadequate layout and 50 years later exploded into a quadruple-track interchange on the edge of a veritable 'Spaghetti Junction' of exquisitely logical curves. Another 50 years and 'logic' dictated that the place be turned into a derelict wilderness.

The remarkable thing about junction station life was its continuity, the way the trains and the train service remained recognisably the same over two or even three generations so that both they and the junction station itself became part of the way of life of a community. There were various reasons for the fall from grace of the railway and its junction stations, letting the enemy, road transport, get a foot in the door by going on strike at inopportune moments was one, but in spite of such matters the railway station was always loved by its locals and even car drivers knew it would be there to bale them out when the roads were blocked by snow. Some junctions were more useful than others but in the crazy, road-jammed situation of the late 1980s who would dare to say that we do not need them back again. We need all the transport we can get.

Acknowledgements

A book such as this takes a massive input of research — most of which was carried out at the Public Record Office, Kew, and I would like to thank the staff there for their friendly help. There is the slightest tendency these days for readers to be turned out before the appointed hour — but let that pass, inebriates in a public house complain when the landlord calls 'Time!'. I should also like to thank Mr R. A. Cooke of Harwell for his generous help by telephone and letter concerning station layouts, opening and closing dates and last but by no means least I must acknowledge the assistance I was given by the Signalling Record Society without whose careful researches this book would be the poorer. I am very pleased to have the opportunity to thank my good friends David Collins, Larry Crosier, Reg Instone and John Morris for their invaluable help with historic data on signal boxes. Anyone wishing to know more about the Society should contact the Membership Secretary, 18 Boston Avenue, Reading RG1 5LY.

Adrian Vaughan
Barney 1987

Castle Cary

Castle Cary station lies on a plain at the foot of the hill on which stands the little market town of the same name. The station was built on the west side of the road running north from the town towards Evercreech and Shepton Mallet, the lane crossing the railway on the level. The station offices were very simply built of local Kineton stone to the designs of J. P. Brereton, one of Brunel's assistants. The station opened on 1 September 1856 as part of the Great Western's wonderfully wayward route from Thingley Junction, 2 miles west of Chippenham on the Paddington-Bristol main line, to Weymouth. The works began grandly enough, in the shape of a double track, broad gauge railway to Westbury, opened on 5 September 1848; but thereafter the work proceeded slowly and as cheaply as possible with many curves and steep gradients — the earthworks and bridge were laid for double track but only a single line of rails went west and southwest, opening to Frome on 7 October 1850, to Yeovil Pen Mill on 1 September 1856 and to Weymouth on 20 January 1857.

The broad gauge single track was one of the first to be operated by means of the new-fangled electric telegraph — the clerk or policeman at each station used the telegraph to come to an agreement as to which train was to go forward into their single-track section. The system was not underwritten by any form of train staff but with the sparse traffic of those days seems to have survived without head-on collisions.

The gauge was changed to the standard, Stephenson, 4ft 8½in during the week 18-26 July 1874 and during 1880-81 it was converted to double track using steel rails on longitudinal sleepers. The double line of rails reached Castle Cary in June or July 1880. On 21 July Col Yorke inspected the new layout for the Board of Trade and passed it fit for use. A signalbox had been erected at the station during or before 1875 and the signalman here had

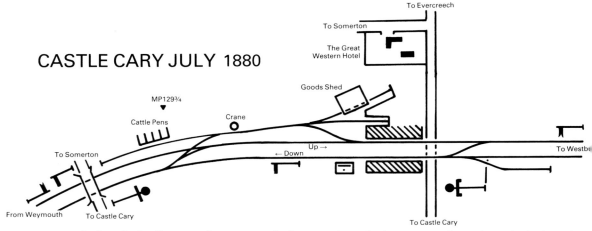

CASTLE CARY JULY 1880

operated the single line to the east and the southwest with block telegraph instruments but no staff, if the working timetable is to be taken literally according to the words printed therein. After the doubling of the track the block telegraph was used in a more familiar way for the signalling of up and down trains. The up and down home signals were of the disc and crossbar type, the one for the up line being sited high up on the cutting side on the inside of the curve and therefore presumably being visible from the distant signal or even before that. The down distant signal was set ¾-mile away from the station and, with the long straight track leading to the station, this and its home signal would have been plainly visible from a long way off. When brakes were poor, signal siting had to be very good.

Castle Cary remained the junction between single and double track working until November 1881 when the doubling of the track was completed through Sparkford to Yeovil Pen Mill. On 12 November Col Yolland came down to inspect the new line for the Board of Trade and passed it as safe but not before he had criticised the GWR for having such short platforms at Castle Cary (300ft). 'I can only hope there will not be an accident as a result', he grumbled. He also found the GWR remiss in that no change-of-gradient signs had been provided. 'Every company does this, even the Great Western on the rest of their system, and I do not see why an exception should be made in this instance.'

Castle Cary station was a wayside place with a slowly developing traffic passing through and calling at it. The service of 'all stations' passenger trains of 1865 was still practically the same in 1875. There were no express trains — most services ran between Bristol or Chippenham and Weymouth, with just two or three through trains from Paddington to Weymouth and back, stopping at just about every station. Slow goods trains stopped to attach and detach agricultural produce including

cattle and of course coal was brought in by rail. Milk, carried in churns — or 'cans' as the GWR called them — developed as a traffic for London from the early 1880s, thus providing a new market for the farmers around the Castle Cary district and a new smell for the railway atmosphere — that of sour milk in the returned empty cans. The only claim to fame for the little station was that of stabling banking engines for the Bruton incline. Eastwards from Castle Cary the line fell briefly at 1 in 100 and then commenced the 4½-mile climb over the Mendips on gradients of 1 in 90 and 1 in 80 to the summit at Milepost 122¾. Banking power from Castle Cary was provided from Yeovil shed but does not appear to have been needed for many trains if the working timetables are any guide. When special trains of freight, not shown in the timetables, were run, there may have been extra banking required. Passenger trains were never banked up Bruton. If assistance was required the additional engine would have been placed ahead of the train engine as a pilot.

In 1900 the new, ambitious spirit of the Great Western management showed itself in the earthworks of the Stert cut-off, a new, high-speed railway running from the Hungerford to Devizes line at Patney & Chirton to Westbury, which reduced the distance between Paddington, Westbury and all points west by no less than 14½ miles. With this a modest service of fast trains hauled by powerful 2-4-0 locomotives was instituted, calling at main line stations only. Castle Cary saw its first non-stop expresses from 1900. In 1903 work commenced on the Somerton cut-off. commencing at Milepost 129¾ at Castle Cary, a new line was dug, tunnelled and embanked 22¾ miles to a junction with the old 'Great Way Round' at Cogload, 4¾ miles east of Taunton. In only three years the line, heavily engineered and with five stations, was opened to passenger traffic. What was the effect on Castle Cary station of being promoted to a junction? The platforms, criticised

Right:
Castle Cary station date unknown but probably shortly after the doubling of the line in 1880-81. Note that the up platform office seems little bigger than the downside waiting shed. The upside office was extended during 1880 to include a 'Ladies' Room' and an enclosed lavatory for men. The goods shed can be seen behind the group of men on the up platform and the signalbox is on the downside, just off the platform end.
Author's Collection

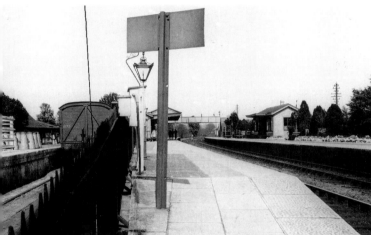

Left:
Looking east along the up platform in 1922. The milk dock and cattle pens are on the left with a Siphon milk churn wagon and some neatly placed churns. *L&GRP (8729)*

Below:
Castle Cary station seen from the bridge over the Weymouth line in 1922. The hipped-roof signalbox and spacious goods shed were built to standard designs laid down around 1896 and constructed here during 1903-07. *L&GRP*

by Col Yolland in 1881, were extended eastwards 120ft, blocking the level crossing and necessitating the provision of a footbridge. An ornate, cast-iron 'Gentlemen's convenience' was erected on the down platform and another for both sexes on the up side. The old goods shed was demolished and a larger one was erected to the standard, brick design, behind the new signalbox at Milepost 129¾. The resiting of the goods shed enabled a more spacious layout to be provided in the goods yard. The new signalbox was to the then standard, brick pattern with a hip gabled roof and housed a frame of 55 levers, of which 44 were in use and 11 were spare.

The effect of the new line on the revenue-earning capabilities of the station was ambiguous as the table below demonstrates. The income shown is that for all passenger business — freight income is not known. The statistics come, of course, from GWR records.

| | Staff | Paybill £ | Income £ | Tickets | General merchandise | | Cattle fwd |
					Fwd (tons)	Rec (tons)	
1903	11	662	15,105	16,722	2,126	11,923	435
1913	13	974	12,596	20,307	2,700	4,891	491

Left:
Castle Cary seen in 1947 from almost the same spot as in the preceding photograph. The wartime ARP signalbox is an obvious alteration while the fine goods shed is conspicuous by its absence. One wall remains after the bombing raid of 1942 but the loading platform is open to the sky. On the Weymouth loop a ringed-arm signal has replaced the ground disc and a banner repeater has been provided to give drivers advance information on the aspect of a signal out of sight around the bend behind the camera. *L&GRP (12162)*

Right:
The view looking east from the window of Castle Cary signalbox in 1953 as 'Hall' 4-6-0 No 4978 *Westwood Hall* brings a down passenger working through with all the impetus gained from the descent of Bruton Bank. The signal for the Taunton line is lowered; next to it on the bracket is the Weymouth line signal and on the right of that the signal for the short goods loop. *Author*

10

Right:
On 2 July 1955, 'Hall' 4-6-0 No 4917 *Crosswood Hall* passes the down junction signal at Castle Cary with an up express. The loop starting signal has a ringed arm and a route indicator, the latter taking the place of an extra signal arm on a bracket.
R. C. Riley (55/39)

Below:
No 8744, a Westbury-allocated '57XX' 0-6-0PT, waits on the short loop at Castle Cary, ready to reverse its 'B' set into the platform to form a local service to Taunton via Somerton on 22 July 1958.
R. C. Riley

Bottom:
BR Standard '5' 4-6-0 No 73029, a Swindon engine, takes an 'H' headcode freight round the curving junction for Yeovil and Weymouth on 7 July 1959.   *R. C. Riley (13782)*

With the opening of the new line the signalman saw more trains pass his signalbox at speed, the service increasing as the years passed, but even in 1910 the 'New Line' was not scheduled to be busy with regular trains. There were however the seasonal excursions and the almost daily 'Ocean Liner' expresses to boost the booked total. In 1910 51 trains of all sorts were scheduled to pass through Castle Cary. Seven were West of England expresses like the 'Cornish Riviera' or the 10.20am Kingswear, two were non-stop expresses on the Weymouth service, a couple more were fully vacuum braked goods trains out of Cornwall but the rest were stopping passenger trains, long-distance freights which called at the station, local 'Fly' goods and steam railmotors servicing the 'New Line'.

The signalman at Castle Cary in 1910 saw plenty of action even though he did not handle a large number of trains. Five down goods trains stopped to work at the station and another was scheduled to be back-shunted to the down refuge to clear the road to Taunton for the 'Cornish Riviera'. On the up line a series of 'K' headcode 'Fly' goods worked a complicated pattern to service the rambling routes of the area. The 6.15am Yeovil Pen Mill worked at Castle Cary from 6.50 to 7.30am, ran to Somerton — where it dropped off the Somerton station truck which had earlier been detached from a Swindon to Weymouth goods — and then returned at 8.35am for all stations to Swindon, shunting at each one. The men working these trips were 'double home men' in many cases yet only covering a relatively short mileage. The station truck system was a very old-established practice on GWR in 1910 whereby a specially branded covered van worked from one station to another carrying some important traffic, usually perishables. The Somerton truck — 'ST 40' — worked to Paddington and might have carried high class groceries for shops in Somerton. In the afternoon a goods left Yeovil for Radstock and Bristol, calling at Castle Cary to pick up traffic, and at about the same time another trip left Yeovil for Castle Cary via Monacute, arriving at Castle Cary, therefore, from the Taunton direction. At 6.15pm it had done its business, reversed and left for Bridgwater.

While local 'Fly' goods shunted the yard the passenger service was provided almost entirely by 'B' class trains — locomotives and coaches — and steam railmotors. The only express trains to call were the 12.35pm Weymouth at 1.04pm and the 5pm Paddington at 7.40pm. One of the down stopping services was one of those tricky trains that the GWR persisted in running so that the old ideal of the 'Great Way Round' should not be forgotten — a Chippenham to Taunton service going via Yeovil. The railmotors serviced the wayside station on the new line and were obviously not supposed to do more. They worked into Castle Cary, reversed and returned whence they came, to Durston or Bridgwater and sometimes to Taunton. Occasionally too, they made connections into or out of the longer distance trains. A passenger for Somerton on the 6am Paddington arriving at Castle Cary at 8am had only to wait half an hour for the following railmotor to take him to his destination. In the evening, people from the 'New Line' stations came to Castle Cary on the 6.50pm railmotor from Bridgwater and after a 20min wait caught the 6.17 from Weymouth to Swindon. There were five 'motors' in each direction over the Somerton line. One of them missed obvious connections by only a few minutes, another merely arrived, reversed and departed after a short break without any connection at all. In 1910 no freight train was scheduled to take on a banker but in 1929, out of 15 up freights, five were timed to stop for this purpose. The 1910 service pattern at Castle Cary was reinforced by there being more express trains to the west and to Weymouth — 19 in all, 10 of them on the Weymouth line. Passenger business seemed to be of more importance in this area than it had been 20 years before, passenger and fast freight, fully fitted goods and heavy, milk tanker trains, while the steam railmotors on the Somerton line service had been replaced by an 'auto' or 'push-pull' train at the same frequency. The early 20th century pattern continued, the train service improved, diesel railcars were put on to the Bristol-Weymouth service almost as soon as they were introduced to the GWR, the excitement of the railway increased, only the revenue, the amount of traffic carried, declined as the table below shows.

| | Staff | Paybill £ | Income £ | Tickets | General merchandise | | Cattle fwd |
					Fwd (tons)	Rec (tons)	
1923	17	2,824	18,317	10,653 (59)	2,102	3,966	222
1929	18	2,865	19,014	19,669 (47)	1,995	3,654	213
1930	18	2,934	17,958	18,874 (67)	1,660	4,128	200
1933	17	2,830	14,575	17,012 (79)	1,071	3,827	156
1938	19	2,893	12,079	16,361 (58)	1,039	3,952	122

(Figures in brackets are season tickets sold.)

Left:
BR 'Britannia' Pacific No 70027 *Rising Star* hurries through Castle Cary station towards Bruton Bank with the 9.20am (SO) from St Ives to Paddington on 2 July 1955. The 1856 stone buildings with the canopy dating from around 1880 and the typical GWR corrugated iron shed for a parcels office. *R. C. Riley*

Above:
Castle Cary station looking east from the lampman's platform of the junction signal in 1973. A GWR backing signal can be seen on the platform on the left. The ruins of what was once a beautiful garden on the down platform are evident on the right. At the right-hand end of the footbridge are stairs leading down to the old road or path which once made a level crossing here; the hedge marks its further southwards course. *Author*

Left:
A 1974 view from the down goods loop, looking west. Nearest the camera is the down loop to main starting signal. The other tall signal is the down main inner home and framed between them is the starter signal bracket for up main and loop lines. *John Morris*

13

Above:
A 1970 view looking east from the Westbury end of the up platform, with a train signalled on down main.   *Reg Farrell*

Left:
Looking west from the Taunton end of up platform in 1970. Note the GWR backing signal which is equipped with a route indicator capable of showing three routes — 'WEY', 'TNTN', and 'SDG' — in conjunction with the lowered arm. The signalbox can be seen beyond the signal post.   *Reg Farrell*

Below:
Castle Cary's very unprepossessing signalbox, constructed in the 'ARP' style of 1942, photographed in 1970. Note that the traditional double junction has been replaced by the modern version using only 'single leads'.   *Reg Farrell*

It is important to know, when looking at the income figures, that, relative to 1913 fares, there had been a 50% increase in 1923, 1924, 1926 and 1927 whilst the rates for carrying parcels, coal and general merchandise went up at the same time by the same or even larger amounts up to 75% in one increase. The difficulties the Great Western faced from road transport can be deduced from the figures above with wages relatively stable in spite of staff increases but income fallling along with the amount of traffic generated by the station.

On 3 September 1942 Signalman Silbey was in Castle Cary box on early turn. The Yeovil to Durston 'Fly' goods was performing its time-honoured ceremonies in the station when four bombs fell at 9.14am. One made a direct hit on the signalbox, killing Mr Silbey. Another fell alongside the engine of the 'Fly', No 1729, chewing it to tatters and killing the driver, Mr Shergold. A third is said to have passed horizontally through the bar of the Great Western Hotel. The pilot machine-gunned the area and flew away having celebrated the third anniversary of the outbreak of the war by killing six harmless people. By 11pm the same night the track had been sufficiently repaired to permit single line working and in a few days the working returned to normal although the double junction was controlled from a small, shack-like signalbox brought down from Reading signal works, one of a small stock of spare signalboxes kept for such emergencies. A new brick signalbox to the then standard ARP (Air Raid Precautions) design with a frame of 85 levers was brought into use on 27 November 1942. Many of these were spare levers but they were all in use from 28 March 1943 to control the enlarged layout of goods loops and sidings.

After the terrors of war, the railway subsided to the level of activity it had known in the late 1920s and through the 1930s, certainly as far as Castle Cary was concerned. The pattern of service was that of 1910 with locomotive and carriage stock dating from the 1920s and 1930s. Even the 'dashers', the 14xx and trailer, continued to scamper up and down the Somerton line and indeed, in 1955 all five made good connections at Castle Cary with up and down Weymouth line trains. In this respect the service was better than it had been 45 years earlier. Passenger trains were more numerous; several of the services were provided by diesel railcars of GWR design though they do not appear to have been used on the Somerton line. Freight trains ran in good numbers but the network of 'Fly' goods was greatly reduced. The local 'pick-up' still ran but the accent was on greater speed and longer distance trains.

The first actual, total loss of service was the abolition of the Somerton line service when the stations on the line shut down on 10 September 1962. Diesel locomotives took over more and more trains at the same time that the total number was reduced. The first track to be removed at Castle Cary since the 1880s was lifted on 15 December 1963 when the facing points from the down main to the short down loop alongside the Weymouth line were removed along with the up Weymouth line refuge siding. The connections from the goods yard to the down Taunton line went between March and May 1968 and the rest of those sidings in the yard were taken out in 1970. The Weymouth line was singled on 12 May 1968. The signalbox was closed on 3 February 1985 and the completely revamped layout came under the control of a man in Westbury Panel signalbox. The station remains, and is served by DMUs on the Weymouth-Bristol/Cardiff service and by High Speed Trains on the Paddington-West of England run.

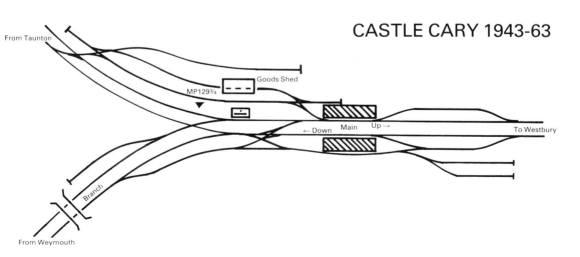

CASTLE CARY 1943-63

From Taunton

Goods Shed

MP129¾

←Down Main Up→ To Westbury

Branch

From Weymouth

Top:
The 16.15 Weymouth-Bristol DMU enters the up platform at Castle Cary in 1973 by way of the main to main crossover — the other part of the modern junction at this location. *Author*

Above:
The original down platform waiting shelter at Castle Cary — an 1856 design typical of the Wilts, Somerset & Weymouth Railway buildings west of Westbury. Note the nice, late Victorian or Edwardian GWR platform seats. Photographed in 1973. *Author*

Left:
Gas lamp, gent's urinal dating from 1880 and a glimpse of the 1852 waiting room behind, the 1942 signal and signalbox in the distance. Taken in June 1973. *Author*

Hatton

Hatton station was opened as part of the Great Western's Oxford to Birmingham line — a double track, mixed gauge (7ft 0¼in and 4ft 8½in) railway opened on 1 October 1852. The station stood 112¼ miles from Paddington, via Oxford, close to the Grand Union canal and about 2 miles from several small villages. The countryside was hilly, wooded and very pleasant. The station stood on a short length of level track in what was otherwise an unbroken climb at 1 in 95/1 in 110 from near Warwick, 4¾ miles away, to a point about a mile north of the station; banking engines were consequently very much part of the life of Hatton.

The station buildings were simple single-storey offices. On the down platform the main office was in brick with plain gables, dating in all probability from 1852 though with a later canopy from, perhaps, 1897. On the upside there was a simple, wooden waiting shelter with an outline very similar to that built in stone at Castle Cary and with the same inadequate design of canopy dating from the 1850s. Some GWR corrugated iron sheds were erected on each side of this building.

Hatton station became a junction on 10 October 1860 when the Stratford-on-Avon Railway Company (SRC) opened its 9½-mile, single track, mixed gauge railway to a terminus on the northwest side of that town. It was a curious route.

Above:
Hatton station — the view towards Leamington in about 1933. The station nameboard informs travellers that this is 'Hatton, Junction for Bearley, Alcester and Stratford-on-Avon'. The old South signalbox, dating from 1880 or earlier can be seen in the distance. *P. A. Hopkins*

The obvious course ran southwest from Warwick up the Avon valley — a distance of 10 miles at most — but perhaps the land could not be purchased. As it turned out, trains passed Warwick westwards and worked very hard to climb out of the Avon valley for nearly 5 miles before turning off at Hatton on a 9-mile downhill run back into the same valley at Stratford. This was the second railway into Shakespeare's town. Half a mile to the south lay the terminus of the Oxford, Worcester & Wolverhampton Railway's (OWWR) branch from Honeybourne. On 24 July 1861 a link line about 700yd long was opened from the SRC's line to the terminus of the OWWR branch. The terminus then became a through station and a train service commenced at once linking Leamington with Worcester through Hatton. GWR broad gauge trains continued to operate between Leamington, Hatton and the SRC's terminus but after 18 months this curious duplication was abandoned and thereafter it is doubtful if any broad gauge trains used the branch. On 1 April 1869 the entire main line from Oxford to Wolverhampton was converted to standard gauge operation alone and from that time Hatton ceased to see any of Gooch's 'eight-footers' or their even more splendid 4-4-0 brethren.

Hatton station served as a junction for Stratford-on-Avon more for up trains than for down workings. Passengers for Stratford from the north would have changed trains at Hatton but travellers coming up from the south would have changed at Leamington. In 1875 the 9.30am, 11.40am and 3pm Wolverhampton to Paddington expresses slipped a coach for Stratford at Hatton. This was a fairly adventurous activity in those days. The train was running on a 1 in 171 falling gradient and the slip guard had only his handbrake with which to bring the coach to a stand. The hoary old legend of the stationmaster's remark to the slip guard — 'you stop where you can and I'll wheel the station out to meet you' — probably had its genesis at Hatton. Down expresses from London invariably slipped the Stratford coach at Leamington where it was shunted to the branch train to follow the express up the bank a few minutes later; in this respect Leamington, not Hatton was the junction for Stratford.

The layout at Hatton prior to 1897 was an awkward one to operate because there were no facing points in the main line to the branch. The station was worked by 'South' and 'North' signalboxes, both on the down side and each about 50yd off the platform ends, the North box being in the 'V' of the junction. Any train for Stratford had to be reversed from the down platform to a siding and then drawn forward alongside the branch platform, this being the rear face of the down main platform. This lack of facing points was standard practice when the branch was built and facing point bolts were unknown, causing railway managements to have a horror of facing junctions in high speed main lines. That there were still no facing points at Hatton in 1896 shows the lethargy into which the Great Western had fallen. Trains from Stratford met facing points — but they were only branch trains. They could run across to the up main platform or along the branch platform and gain the up main at the South box. The branch line was regulated from Hatton North, a 31-lever box, by means of the Train Staff and Ticket system. The block section was Hatton North to Bearley Junction, the staff a short length of wood, triangular in section, painted blue; from Bearley Junction to Stratford the staff was a piece of cylindrically shaped wood, painted red.

Hatton saw more and more trains as the years passed and the branch line became not just the route for Leamington-Stratford locals, or longer-distance trains either to Honeybourne, Evesham or Worcester, but also an important freight link between Banbury and South Wales, giving an alternative path for London-South Wales traffic as the old main line became crowded. By 1895 there were five down expresses from Paddington with a through coach for Stratford, the latter being slipped at Leamington in each case. Three more coaches were slipped at Hatton off up expresses. There was one Worcester to Birmingham train and another from Stourbridge, via Birmingham, which reversed at Hatton for Stourbridge — hence the need for the turntable behind the branch platform. The Worcester to Birmingham service came in from Stratford and thus the engine was facing Leamington and had to be turned. The Stour-

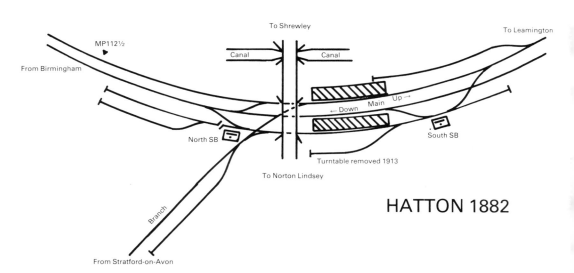

HATTON 1882

18

Above:
The main office building seen about 1955. The new South signalbox is on the platform between the office and the footbridge. *M. J. Lewis*

Below:
The offices on the up platform, dating from c1852, surrounded by the type of corrugated iron sheds for which the GWR was famous. *M. J. Lewis*

Left:
'Castle' 4-6-0 No 5080 *Defiant* passes Hatton West Junction's up home signals with a down express for Bristol and the West of England via Stratford-on-Avon in about 1959. The signalbox can just be seen behind some bushes. From left to right the signal arms route, to the down goods loop (on the Hatton North curve), to Hatton North curve, and to Hatton South. The relevant boxes' fixed distants are below the stop arms. Note the GWR wooden posts. *Author's Collection*

Centre left:
Hatton station viewed from the road bridge in about 1959 with the branch line platform nearest the camera. *M. J. Lewis*

Bottom left:
The station from the road bridge looking down the approach lane in the Leamington direction to the up main platform in about 1959. *M. J. Lewis*

Top:
A view from the footbridge looking north. The branch can be seen bearing left through the old stone arch of the road bridge. A GWR wooden signal bracket stands on the left — note the small arm low down routeing to the down sidings — and a BRWR tubular steel junction signal can be seen on the main line to the right. The stop blocks mark the location of the one-time turntable siding close to the gangers' hut. *M. J. Lewis*

Above:
Still on the footbridge, looking north as Ivatt '2MT' 2-6-0 No 46505 gallops off the branch line with a full head of steam, bound for Leamington. The engine had worked a goods train to Stratford. *M. J. Lewis*

bridge to Stourbridge via Snow Hill also had to turn its engine. The up slip coaches had to be retrieved from the up platform and brought to the down side for attaching to the branch train. If the passengers were to remain in their seats — which was the whole idea of slipping coaches — then all points facing the movement had to be clamped tight shut by the porter using cast-iron 'G' clamps and padlocks. This took extra time on a very busy main line.

The Great Western scheduled many awkward movements in their efforts to provide a good train service and in the absence of proper layouts the management depended upon the skill of its staff to carry out difficult manoeuvres quickly and safely. The railway in those days was never afraid to *handle* trains and Hatton, with its slip coaches, freight shunting, bank engines, engine turning and running-round must have had a very capable staff.

While all this was undoubtedly in the heroic mould of railway *work*, it was not necessarily good railway *practice*. From 1890 the Great Western was under a new and ambitious management which was anxious to direct the heroism of its staff along more remunerative lines, and in that decade was laid the groundwork for the enormous expansion of the first decade of the 20th century. In August 1894 the GWR purchased land at Hatton for the purpose of laying a southeast to northwest loop, connecting the Stratford branch with the main line, the junction facing Birmingham about ½ mile north of Hatton station. The loop was laid as a double track railway and at the same time the layout at Hatton North box was improved and realigned. The branch from Hatton North to the new junction with the loop line was doubled and the curve was eased, passing over the site of the old North box and making a normal double junction with the main line, the points facing Leamington. A new site in the 'V' of the junction was created by filling and a new signalbox of 55 levers was built. This was named Hatton Middle. Hatton North Junction was the 25-lever (18 working, 7 spare) signalbox working the junctions to and from the loop line. Where the loop met the line to Stratford out of Hatton station the junction was controlled by a 21-lever box called Hatton Branch Junction.

All this new work was inspected and passed as safe for use by the Board of Trade's Inspector on 23 July 1897. Now the Birmingham-Worcester trains did not have to reverse at Hatton but, even more important, a strategic link had been made for the future which the GWR was planning. On 1 August 1906 the line from Honeybourne East Junction to Cheltenham was opened throughout to passenger trains and the Hatton loop began to carry some really long-distance traffic between Birmingham, South Wales, Bristol and the West of England. As early as 1901 a down goods loop had had to be laid alongside the loop so the traffic was heavy.

However, the importance of the link was short-lived for on 1 July 1908 the Birmingham & North Warwickshire Railway was opened from Tyseley, 3½ miles south of Birmingham, to the Stratford line at Bearley Junction. The old single track branch southwards from Bearley was doubled and this became the GWR's main route from the Midlands to the West and to South Wales. Hatton loop was short-circuited, the branch from Bearley to Hatton Branch Junction remained single track and only a very few long-distance trains used the line thereafter — the occasional, daily train to Worcester or a South Wales freight that would not fit into the timetable on the Tyseley line. In the 1930s the 9am Birmingham to Stratford diesel railcar went via Hatton to clear the North Warwickshire line for the fast 9.05am Birmingham to Cardiff train. Of course the loop always remained useful for seasonal extras and summer Saturday trains.

Until January 1937 the working at Hatton was complicated by the division of the layout between the Middle and South boxes. This showed especially on the branch platform which was worked as a single line between the two boxes but without the protection of a single line token or an Acceptance lever. The GWR probably got away with this because it was unlikely that two passenger trains would approach simultaneously along it — up branch trains went to the branch platform while down branch trains used the down main face of that same platform but, even so, owing to shunting movements, the placing of slip coaches on branch trains and other passenger shunting evolutions there were frequent occasions when the branch platform road had to be worked from either end. Safety depended on the care and co-operation of the two signalmen, the trainmen and station staff. When an up branch train — one from Stratford — had to run to the branch platform the Middle signalman 'asked the road' for it in the usual way on the block bell and, if the line was clear to the facing point leading from the platform to the up main line, the South box signalman gave the road. When the branch train was in the platform and another vehicle had to be shunted on to that train from — say — the Middle box, the signalman there sent the 3-4 bell code to South box meaning: 'Take slot off backing signal to allow a train to reverse to branch platform and vehicles already there.' When the South box signalman pulled his slot off the Middle box signal, Middle could lower that and then go to the window with a green flag or lamp as a warning to the driver to be cautious. On the engine rode a porter to conduct the driver to the train in the platform.

On 8 January 1937 the Great Western, at a stroke, simplified and made safer the working at Hatton whilst also reducing costs. The old South box was abolished and a new South box, taking over from the old Middle and South boxes, was opened on the Birmingham end of the down platform. This had 84 levers — 74 working and 10 spares. The regulations still urged extreme caution on drivers entering the Branch platform from Stratford, but now the single track was under one man's control and was that bit safer. Since 1903 Hatton had enjoyed an almost continuous growth in the passenger and freight traffic actually being generated by the station. Only after 1933 did both incoming and outgoing freight traffic fall away, but passenger traffic went from strength to strength to the end of available GWR records, as shown below.

	Staff	Paybill £	Income £	Tickets	General merchandise Fwd (tons)	Rec (tons)	Cattle fwd
1903	17	1,079	3,081	17,551	468	1,314	55
1913	17	1,195	3,671	19,447 (61)	408	1,319	111
1923	19	2,146	6,710	20,354 (387)	438	1,482	68
1929	18	3,006	7,320	20,854 (584)	210	1,425	132
1930	18	3,022	6,033	18,912 (892)	376	1,111	136
1933	18	2,867	4,636	23,881 (583)	374	756	57
1938	16	2,534	4,091	24,743 (357)	55	513	18

Below:
Hatton Junctions looking north from the road bridge in about 1959. Two vans among the weeds in the 'V' of the junction roughly mark the site of the old North box which was abolished in 1937. The curve linking the West and North Junctions runs just beyond the line of trees in the middle distance. *M. J. Lewis*

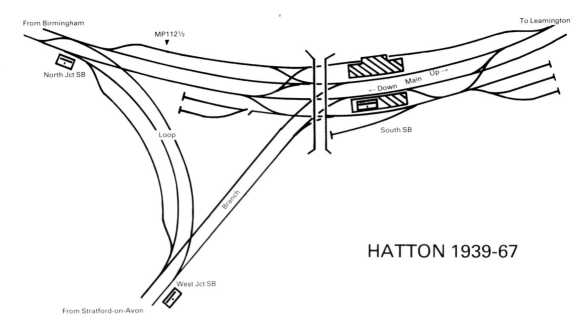

From Birmingham

MP112½

North Jct SB

Loop

Branch

West Jct SB

From Stratford-on-Avon

To Leamington

← Down Main Up →

South SB

HATTON 1939-67

In July 1939 the branch between Bearley and Hatton Branch Junction was opened as double track and the latter signalbox was renamed Hatton West Junction. The name Hatton is, for most railway enthusiasts, synonymous with 'The Bank' and for most of its life the station saw the stirring sight of hard-working goods engines blasting through on the down line, dragging heavy rakes of lumbering wagons and assisted in the rear by a stalwart banking engine, for many years a 2-6-2T of the '51xx' variety. Trains coming up the bank from Stratford — which was even steeper than Hatton Bank and not half as well known to enthusiasts — were frequently assisted in the rear. The train would be brought to a stand at Hatton Middle (later Hatton South) home signal on the branch so that the banking engine could be uncoupled from the rear and sent back to Stratford by the Hatton Branch Junction (later Hatton West Junction) signalman. On the down main line trains

Bottom left:
'Hall' 4-6-0 No 4902 *Aldenham Hall* passes the site of the old South signalbox in about 1953. An ex-LMS '4F' 0-6-0 is standing in the down loop. *R. S. Carpenter*

Right:
'King' 4-6-0 No 6013 *King Henry VIII* passes Hatton on the 4.30pm Wolverhampton-Paddington express on Sunday 22 July 1956. The engine is on drifting steam because there is a 60mph speed restriction over the junction for up trains. *M. Mensing*

Below:
Churchward '43XX' 2-6-0 No 6387 brings a freight train off the Stratford line, through the station, past a row of cottages for railway staff on 23 September 1957. *M. Mensing*

were assisted in the rear from Warwick and the banker was not coupled. It shoved away at the back and finally dropped off when the train engine had reached the summit. If one thinks about this for a moment it will become apparent that considerable skill was required to disengage the banker from the train. The bank engine took half the weight of the wagons so it was no good merely stopping because the rear half of the train would be closed up with the couplings slack and would run backwards until they were taut. In the meantime the front of the train would still be advancing. There would thus be a violent snatch with a considerable risk of coupling breakage. The locomen were handling 70 tons of locomotive and hundreds of tons of train with considerable delicacy — for most of the time at any rate.

On 26 January 1944 the 11.05pm Paddington to Oxley goods took the banker, 2-6-2T No 5184, from Warwick. The early winter morning was very dark as the engines came storming through Hatton at 7.05am. No 5184 dropped-off the train 200yd beyond Hatton North Junction and came back quietly to the ground signal at the crossover, waiting to be crossed to the up main line for the return trip to Warwick.

While the men on the engine waited, the 1.20am Blowers Green to Banbury goods rumbled past them on the up main and turned into the up goods loop. The Hatton North Junction signalman saw the tail lamp, gave 'Train out of Section' to Rowington Junction and accepted the 6.20am Birmingham to Leamington passenger train. He got the road from South box and pulled off. No 5184 was standing on the down main line alongside the up main home signal, but so close that the driver could not see it. He saw the starting signal change to green up ahead and, forgetting to look at his ground signal, set off at a brisk pace.

The Hatton North Junction signalman was at his desk booking all the recent movements when he heard No 5184 move. In his own words he 'flew to the window', gave a red light and shouted 'Whoa!' but the driver did not hear although he passed within a few feet of the window. The signalman then rushed to the bell and sent 2-5-5 'Train or vehicles running away on wrong line' to Hatton South. He also threw his signals back to 'Danger' on the up line. Luckily there was no train signalled on the down line. The Hatton South signalman reversed points Nos 47 and 48 to divert the engine to the branch platform but in his haste he did not look to see where the engine was. It was actually on No 47 points when they were moved and No 5184 was derailed 'all wheels'. The South box signalman heard the crash, realised what had happened and sent 6 bells to Hatton North — 'Obstruction Danger'. In the short time it had taken the signalmen to act, No 5184 had run 660yd and had been travelling fast enough to break the rails and cause one piece to be rammed between a driving wheel and the frame. The Leamington and Tyseley breakdown gangs attended with the Cannock Road steam crane. They arrived at 11.30am and had the engine rerailed at 1.15pm but it took until 3.40pm to remove the lump of rail and thus make the engine mobile. In the meantime, single line working was in force with the inevitable heavy delays to swollen wartime traffic.

The slipping of coaches for Stratford at Hatton did not occur after World War 1. Through coaches from Paddington to Stratford continued to be slipped at Leamington, but their number declined until by 1936 there was but one, off the 9.10am, slipped at Leamington at 10.43am and departing thence to Hatton and Stratford at 10.50am. Note that only 7min were allowed to attach the coach to the branch train. By 1955 there were no coaches

HATTON SOUTH SIGNALBOX DIAGRAM

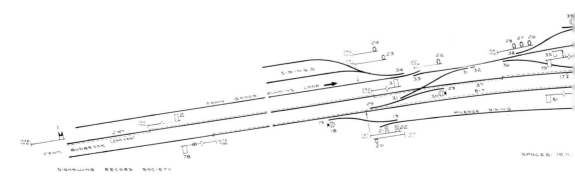

SIGNALLING RECORD SOCIETY

Above:
New age, old railway. 'Western' diesel-hydraulic No D1049
Western Monarch passes the junction at Hatton with the
8.20am Birkenhead to Paddington express on 1 September
1963. Notice the GWR automatic train control ramp in the
down main line by the leading coach. *M. Mensing*

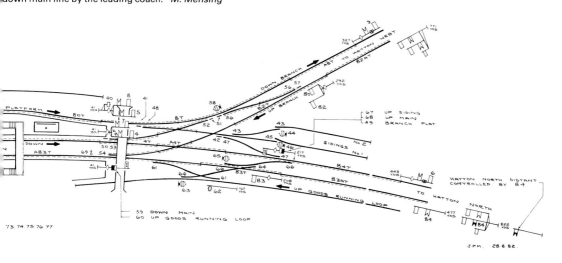

slipped at Leamington for Stratford, but the Hatton South signalman was as busy, if not busier, in 1955 than in 1935. During a summer weekday, the basic train service — excluding excursions — was 160 trains. 'Kings' and 'Castles', with express workings, 'Halls' with rakes of Southern green coaches on the Ramsgate-Birkenhead service, and '28xx' 2-8-0s with 70 wagons banked in the rear came through as heartily and as frequently as they had done for 20 years or more. Eleven goods trains were scheduled to take the banking engine at Warwick. These were mainly iron ore trains running from Banbury to South Wales via Hatton and Honeybourne, but ordinary freight also took assistance, and for every banked train there was the banking engine to cross over and send back downhill again. There were 13 passenger trains to Stratford — eight steam hauled and five formed by ex-GWR diesel railcars; a further railcar working took railway staff from Leamington to Stratford early in the morning.

A train from the down main to the branch required levers 50 and 51 to be pushed 'normal'

into the row of levers thus unbolting facing points 52 and 53. The latter levers were then reversed and rebolted with 50 and 51. Having belled out the 'Is Line Clear?' code to Hatton West, the South box signalman could pull signal levers 9, 7, 3 and 2. To pull off for a down main line train he put those levers back and with levers 50 and 51 reversed he could pull signals 4, 3, 2 and 1. To route a train from up branch to 'back platform' he pushed the bolt levers 57 and 32 into the frame, pulled points 56, 31 and 29, pulled over the bolts, 57 and 32 and lowered signals 78, 79 and 80. Having dispatched that train to Leamington, he put the route back to normal and could 'pull off' on the up main — once he had obtained 'Line Clear' from the Budbrooke signalman. The up main signals were 78, 81, 83 and 84. Between setting up the routes and dismantling them, ringing five or six bell codes per train, booking each one into the register, minute by minute, the signalman at Hatton South was most pleasantly busy. Some periods were busier than others; one, between 7am and 8am had 10 trains scheduled through:

Hatton South 1955

	Working	Classification	Bell code		Time through
5.40am	Wolverhampton-Leamington	'B'	3-1		6.59-7.00am
7.00am	Leamington-Birmingham	'B'	3-1		7.09-7.10am
7.05am	Leamington-Honeybourne	'B'	1-3	To branch	7.17-7.18am
7.02am	Stratford-Leamington	'B'	3-1	From branch	7.22-7.24am
5.45am	Banbury-Severn Tunnel Junction (banked in rear to branch)	'F'	3-2	To branch	7.10-7.27am
6.10am	Wolverhampton-Leamington	'B'	3-1		7.29-7.30am
7.30am	Leamington-Birmingham	'B'	3-1		7.42-7.43am
6.45am	Wolverhampton-Paddington	'A'	4		7.43am
7.23am	Birmingham-Leamington	'B'	3-1		7.58am
7.40am	Stratford-Leamington	'B'	3-1	From branch	8.00-8.02am

Left:
The 10.00am Leamington to Birmingham gets away smartly from Hatton behind 2-6-2T No 4170 on 6 November 1956. *M. Mensing*

Below:
The train that used to slip a coach at Leamington for Stratford. 'King' 4-6-0 No 6024 *King Edward I* heads the 9.10am Paddington to Birkenhead through Hatton on 23 September 1957. *M. Mensing*

The last year in which a freight tonnage was recorded as leaving the station was 1955, the annual total being 92 tons. Passenger figures rose between 1953 and 1959 and the station today remains open as a very useful passenger railhead.

Above:
A view of Honeybourne station looking towards Evesham along the down main platform c1930. *P. A. Hopkins*

Honeybourne

The Oxford, Worcester & Wolverhampton Railway (OWWR) opened the first section of its line from Wolvercote Junction, two miles north of Oxford, to Evesham on 4 June 1853. It was a mixed gauge, single track line with passing loops at stations including Honeybourne. The line climbed steadily northwest over the Cotswolds until, ½-mile beyond Chipping Campden station it tipped over the dramatic Cotswold escarpment on a 1 in 100 incline through the ½-mile-long Campden tunnel to reach level track in about 3¼ miles. Honeybourne station lay about ½-mile west of the foot of the incline, on level track, immediately west of a road bridge at Milepost 101¾ from Paddington, 38¾ miles northwest of Oxford and 4¾ miles east of Evesham. From the outset it was necessary to provide banking assistance on the Campden Bank so a small shed for one engine was provided at the station, on the up side of the line. The OWWR management loathed spending money on the broad gauge which they knew was doomed, but they had obtained Parliamentary permission for their line on the explicit condition that they lay the mixed gauge to accommodate 7ft gauge trains from the GWR. This they did with such reluctance that in all probability the only broad gauge train to use the line was the Board of Trade Inspection special in June 1853. In November that year the OWWR opened a second line of rails to make a double

track from Evesham to Campden but this did not accommodate broad gauge trains and was therefore illegal. The Board of Trade found out about it the following March and banned its use. Single-line working recommenced with Honeybourne as a passing place but on 1 August 1854 the third rail had been added for the non-existent broad gauge trains and Honeybourne finally became a station on a double track railway. Furthermore it was equipped with an electric telegraph instrument, in communication with Campden, for the quicker and safer working of trains on the bank and through the tunnel. This intrusion of the latest technology lay in remote country. The great ridge, known as 'The Edge' for obvious reasons, rose steeply to the east and the hamlets of Cow and Church Honeybourne were the only centres of population.

Honeybourne became a junction on 12 July 1859 when the 9½-mile-long standard gauge single track branch was opened to Stratford-on-Avon. The junction faced Evesham and lay a few feet to the east of the road overbridge. It was a double junction merging at once into a single track which

HONEYBOURNE 1885

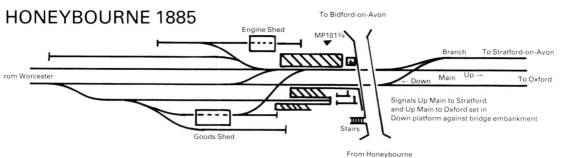

To Bidford-on-Avon

Engine Shed

MP101¾

To Stratford-on-Avon

Branch

from Worcester

←Down   Main   Up→   To Oxford

Signals Up Main to Stratford
and Up Main to Oxford set in
Down platform against bridge embankment

Goods Shed

Stairs

From Honeybourne

Above:
The view towards Oxford from the down platform c1930.
Lens of Sutton

ran parallel to the up main line for ½-mile before gently curving away to the northeast. There was a siding running parallel to the down main line for some distance, so for several hundred yards there was a form of quadruple track. Developments at Stratford and Hatton led to an increase in traffic through Honeybourne and by 1903 it must have been overcrowded with trains and passengers. The figures for 1903 are shown below.

When it is realised that most of Honeybourne's exports took the form of fruit and vegetables, it can be appreciated just how much handling was involved as crates of cabbage or punnets of strawberries were manhandled from horse and cart to railway van. The incoming tonnage was huge and the inference is that the station had developed as the railhead for a wide area of the Vale of Evesham, yet the layout was so small as to be operated by one 31-lever signalbox.

In 1903-04 the Great Western's 'Great Awakening' clanked into Honeybourne in the form of the 'steam navvies' (mechanical excavators) building a new railway from Honeybourne to Cheltenham and widening the Stratford branch for double

Staff	Paybill £	Income £	Tickets	General merchandise Fwd (tons)	Rec (tons)	Cattle fwd
11	608	14,693	17,282	2,471	10,615	142

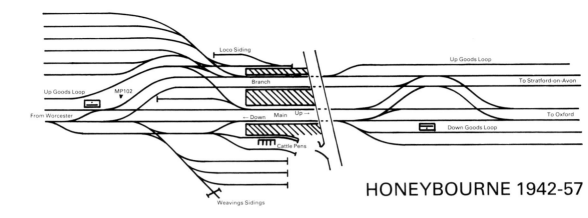

HONEYBOURNE 1942-57

Loco Siding
Up Goods Loop
Branch
To Stratford-on-Avon
Up Goods Loop
MP102
From Worcester
← Down   Main   Up →
To Oxford
Cattle Pens
Down Goods Loop
Weavings Sidings

track. Southwestwards, through the villages below 'The Edge' a fine railway was driven and opened by stages until on 1 August 1906 it had reached the erstwhile terminus of the Gloucester to Cheltenham branch at Cheltenham Malvern Road. The final stage was delayed somewhat when a viaduct fell down between Winchcombe and Bishop's Cleeve. The Stratford line was in effect extended to Cheltenham, passing under the old OWWR line at right angles. To this basic cross-shaped layout, with the original branch line curving into Honeybourne station, was added a curve from the branch to pick up the new line under the bridge facing Cheltenham, and another curve to enable trains from Oxford to join the new line in the direction of Stratford.

The doubling of the branch brought four tracks up to and through the station, after which they merged into the double track line to Evesham at the west end. Here was built Honeybourne Station North signalbox — a brick, hip-roofed building, measuring 38ft×13ft×9ft from rail to floor which housed a 61-lever frame. At the east end of the

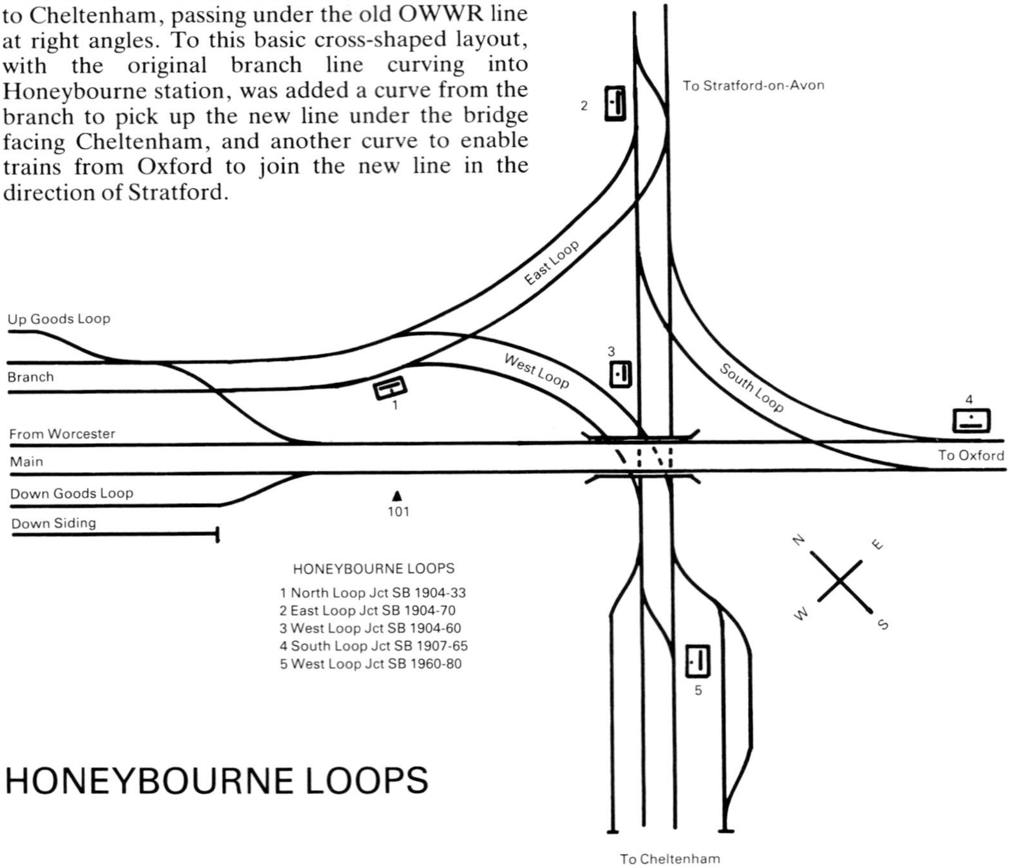

To Stratford-on-Avon

2

East Loop

Up Goods Loop

Branch

West Loop

3

South Loop

4

From Worcester

Main

To Oxford

Down Goods Loop

101

Down Siding

HONEYBOURNE LOOPS

1 North Loop Jct SB 1904-33
2 East Loop Jct SB 1904-70
3 West Loop Jct SB 1904-60
4 South Loop Jct SB 1907-65
5 West Loop Jct SB 1960-80

N
E
W
S

5

HONEYBOURNE LOOPS

To Cheltenham

32

station, controlling double junctions to and from the main lines and branch line, was another signalbox which was identical except that its floor was 11ft above the rails and its lever frame contained 57 levers. Where the curve to Cheltenham diverged from the branch heading to Stratford a timber signalbox (owing to the need for lightness on newly made embankments) was erected. This measured 25ft×12ft×8ft and contained 31 levers. The box was abolished in March 1933 and its function was taken over, by means of power-operated points, by Honeybourne Station South box. Honeybourne East Junction signalbox lay on the new line towards Stratford and was a brick, hip-roofed box measuring 25ft×12ft×9ft 9in which housed a 25-lever frame to work the three-way junction. This box was abolished on 3 November 1970. West Loop signalbox, which was situated close to the OWWR bridge, in the 'V' of the junction between the new line and the curve round from the station, was of identical size to East Loop but was built of timber. On 24 April 1960 this box was abolished and a new West Loop box was opened a few hundred yards to the south, towards Cheltenham.

The opening of the new line brought a great deal of interchange traffic to Honeybourne station and more than doubled the paybill. Unfortunately, income fell dramatically over the ensuing years. Perhaps this was due to traffic being diverted to the new stations on the Honeybourne-Cheltenham section coupled with a slight decline which many stations appear to have suffered during that period. Passenger fares held up remarkably well; it was the loss of outward freight that reduced the station's income.

	Staff	Paybill £	Income £	Tickets	General merchandise Fwd (tons)	Rec (tons)	Cattle fwd
1913	29	1,896	2,975	15,119	2,471	581	209
1923	40	5,881	4,138	18,210 (53)	589	638	161
1929	38	6,037	3,761	15,248 (90)	436	579	338
1930	38	6,029	4,421	15,047 (56)	389	690	373
1933	31	4,983	3,047	13,862 (67)	522	301	170
1938	33	5,510	2,802	17,061 (61)	147	292	157

(Figures in brackets are the number of season tickets sold.)

Above:
'Hall' 4-6-0 No 4918 *Dartington Hall*, built in March 1929, takes water on the up main line while in charge of a summer seasonal train destined for the Devon resorts via Cheltenham. The station nameboard refers to Stratford, Warwick, Leamington, Broadway and Winchcombe but not Birmingham or Cheltenham. *P. A. Hopkins*

33

Honeybourne declined as a railhead but remained important for passengers and as an interchange. It was an expensive luxury. All 'B' class trains called at Honeybourne including those on the 'New' line. There were no direct stopping trains between Stratford and Cheltenham — they all came into Honeybourne where they either reversed or went on to Evesham or Worcester. Those that reversed either returned from whence they had come or continued the journey. Thus a train from Stratford might arrive at Honeybourne and then continue as a train for Cheltenham or vice versa. Originally, all

local services on the Cheltenham-Honeybourne line were operated by steam railmotors while on the Stratford line a railmotor, 'auto-train' (an 0-4-2T and push-pull coach) or conventional train might be found. In the 1920s the steam railmotor was phased out owing to its lack of power and the auto-train took over. This type of train could be driven from a cab at the leading end of the coach and could haul a certain number of vacuum braked freight wagons according to the gradients of the route. In the Vale of Evesham the auto-train, and indeed the little steam railmotor, was frequently

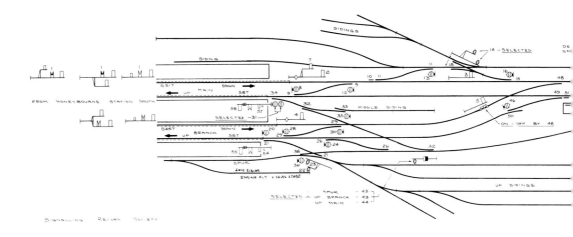

Left:
Looking along the down platform
towards Oxford c1960. *M. J. Lewis*

Right:
Part of the office buildings on the
south end of the down main
platform c1960. In the foreground is
the up main to branch junction
signal. *M. J. Lewis*

seen hauling a couple of covered vans behind the passenger coach. From 1935 diesel railcars, some of which could also haul tail traffic, were introduced both to the Oxford to Worcester and the Stratford to Cheltenham services, but the little 'dasher', the auto-train, held its own and remained in use until 7 March 1960.

Very few 'A' headcode expresses called at Honeybourne at any time in its history. The long-established breakfast-time express from Worcester to Birmingham and the newer, 7.45am Pershore to Birmingham were 'A' class workings and these ran through the 1930s, but by 1955 the Pershore had been discontinued and the Worcester had been reduced to 'B' status. These trains had their return workings, also at 'A' headcode. On the Oxford line in 1908 there was no calling down express neither was there one in 1936 although in that year there was an 'A' class diesel railcar, the 10.20am Oxford which called at 11.10am. On the up line, in 1936, the station was better served. The fast 9.02am Worcester to Paddington called at 9.33 for six minutes and made a connection for Stratford, and the 11.37am Great Malvern to Paddington called at 12.40pm to give connections to London.

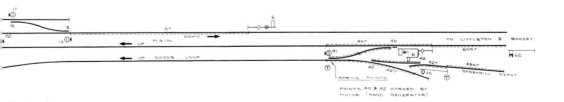

HONEYBOURNE STATION NORTH SIGNALBOX DIAGRAM

HONEYBOURNE STATION SOUTH SIGNALBOX DIAGRAM

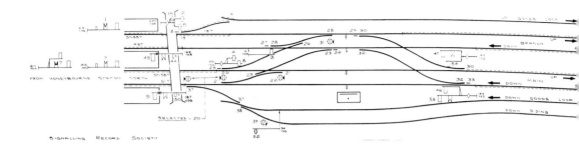

Services to Stratford and Cheltenham were as shown below:

Train	Headcode	Honeybourne arrive/depart
12 noon Stratford-Worcester	'B'	12.18/12.20pm
11.37pm Great Malvern-Paddington	'A'	12.40/12.43pm
To Stratford-on-Avon	—	—/12.50pm
To Cheltenham	—	—/12.55pm

The very fast 12.50pm Hereford to Paddington left Evesham at 2.16pm and ran non-stop to Oxford, a journey of 41¼ miles including Campden and Aston Magna Banks, at an average of 47½mph. Locals wishing to catch this desirable train could do so by boarding the 12.50pm Leamington, engine and coaches, at Honeybourne at 1.55pm due to arrive in Evesham at 2.05pm. One of the longest sequence of interconnections at Honeybourne in the autumn and winter of 1936 occurred each weekday as below:

as well as Honeybourne. The 4.45pm from Paddington had a start-to-stop time of 16min booked for the 15¼ miles from Moreton to Evesham, so it would have been running at about 75mph when it passed Honeybourne at 6.45pm, just about the same time as the 4.10pm Wolverhampton to Paddington went through, pressing on all speed for the climb of Campden Bank. The 6.08pm Oxford-Worcester stopping train had left Oxford 8min after the 4.45pm Paddington had gone, giving 'all stations' connec-

Train	Headcode	Honeybourne arrive/depart
5.55pm Birmingham-Worcester	'A'	6.56/6.58pm
6.45pm Moreton-in-the-Marsh–Cheltenham	'B'	7.05/7.25pm (engine runs round)
6.24pm Cheltenham-Honeybourne auto	'B'	7.22/—
6.08pm Oxford-Worcester	'B'	7.29/7.38pm
7.17pm Stratford-Honeybourne	'B'	7.34/— (engine runs round)
To Stratford	'B'	—/7.45pm

To complete the story hidden in the above table it is necessary to go back an hour. The 5.08pm Cheltenham to Moreton-in-the-Marsh (Headcode 'B'), engine and coaches, arrived at Honeybourne at 5.57pm and left at 6.07pm after the engine had run round. This train formed the 6.45pm 'A' Headcode train from Moreton and followed the crack 4.45pm Paddington to Wolverhampton express. The 6.45pm from Moreton called at Blockley, Campden, Broadway and Gotherington

tions up the Evenlode valley and over the Cotswolds behind the grander train. In total, there were seven passenger trains in the Worcester to Oxford direction and seven in the opposite direction which called at Honeybourne in the course of a weekday in 1936 while there were another 17 trains serving the station from the Cheltenham-Stratford line and, in some but not all cases, making connections at Honeybourne. There was no slip coach service at the station in 1908 or

36

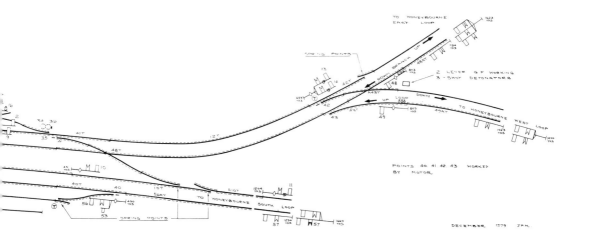

Right:
The station exterior seen from the approach road on the upside c1960. *M. J. Lewis*

Below:
'Castle' 4-6-0 No 7017 *G. J. Churchward* enters Honeybourne station on the up main line with a Hereford-Paddington express in July 1956. The shunters' cabin is on the right and Station North box is just visible behind the GWR wooden bracket signal. *P. Ransome-Wallis*

1910 when slip coaches were at the peak of their fame and usage and there was no such service there in 1936.

There was no turntable at Honeybourne — probably due to the existence of two triangular junctions in the layout — but the lack led to a certain amount of cumbersome or intricate reversing manoeuvres. In the 1930s and later periods, reversals were only undertaken by goods trains — except in special circumstances — and I will pass on to this shortly but first I must include a daily manoeuvre from the Heroic Period of railway operation and the year 1908. The 4.55pm Cheltenham to Moreton-in-the-Marsh arrived at Honeybourne East Junction at 5.46pm and stopped with the tail of the train clear of the crossover. Waiting on the opposite line was the engine for the remainder of the journey. This backed on to the train through the crossover and took it to Moreton via South Junction. An hour later the 6.28pm Kingham arrived at East Junction, facing Stratford, at 6.46pm. An engine

facing Cheltenham was standing on the opposite
line. In 3min (according to the timetable) the train
had been split and the front part had left for
Stratford and after a further 3min the rear part had
a new engine and was on its way to Cheltenham.

The station and outlying junctions handled more
trains as the years passed. For instance in 1908
there were six goods trains running through from
Cheltenham to Stratford and beyond and four
express trains. In 1936 there were, on an autumn
or winter weekday, 15 scheduled expresses and 27
freights running non-stop under the Oxford-
Worcester line at Honeybourne, plus three more
that took the curve from East to South Junction —
each one booked for banking assistance — and five
more goods trains came round the curve in the
opposite direction. A total of 100 trains were
booked to pass, start or terminate at Honeybourne
on the Oxford line including, two freights that
were scheduled to take the banker. In addition,
there would have been light engine movements,
shunting trips around the station and extra
seasonal passenger and freight trains. Only one
freight, the 3.20am Oxford to Severn Tunnel, was
scheduled to reverse at Honeybourne in 1936. In
1955, on a summer weekday, 125 trains were
booked to pass, start from or terminate at the
station, including 17 goods trains, most of which
did shunting work at the station, starting from or
terminating in the sidings. Eight up goods trains
were booked to take the banker. On the 'New' line
there were 43 goods trains in a 24hr day and six
express passenger trains of which three were diesel

railcars. Five more freights took the East to South
Junction curve and all had banking assistance,
while 12 goods and parcels trains used the curve in
the opposite direction. On summer Saturdays
there were 30 express trains scheduled. Two
Oxford to Severn Tunnel Junction freights arrived
on the main line at Honeybourne and reversed
around to the Cheltenham line to continue their
journey. The station and its environs were a hive
of activity as freight and passenger trains shunted.

Several goods trains on the Stratford-
Cheltenham line turned into Honeybourne to pick
up or cut off wagons and over the years there were
a lot of minor derailments. On 21 August 1942
Collett '2251' 0-6-0 No 2294 was driven through
the buffer stops in a siding and on to 'Olde
England' where it languished for many days until
the time could be found to drag it back. On
11 September 1947 at 7.09am, yard staff saw that a
wagon was on fire in a train drawing along the
down goods loop. They hurried to the scene and
found a wagonload of RAF empty petrol tanks in
flames. Very bravely, some unnamed hero got
between the burning wagon and the next,
uncoupled the train behind it and waved the driver
forward to the water column where the flames
were soon doused.

A train from the Oxford direction, requiring to
reverse out to the Cheltenham line (and thus keep
the engine with its chimney leading) was, ideally,
routed from the down main to the down branch
platform by the Honeybourne Station South
signalman. To do this he 'got the road' from

Left:
Looking from the road bridge towards Oxford, Honeybourne Station South box is hidden in the exhaust from '2251' 0-6-0 No 2259. The locomotive is carrying the 'H' headlamp code. The signal is an original 1906 installation with well painted, tapered wooden posts and early pattern pressed steel arms with the old type of spectacles. Even the lamp cases seem to have been polished. The two rectangular boxes on the post, house electrical contacts to operate signal arm repeaters in the signalbox.
P. G. Barlow/Author's Collection

Above right:
'Hall' 4-6-0 No 6913 *Levens Hall* coasts into Honeybourne, past the Station North box, with a train of empty coaches for Stratford in June 1964. With steam shut off the fireman is taking the opportunity to fill the boiler — note the overflow from the injector at footstep level. No 4124, a '51XX' 2-6-2T, is doing some shunting and is probably rostered as banker for the day.
Derek Cross

Right:
Collett '2251' 0-6-0 No 2222 working hard as banker on the Campden incline on 11 April 1964. Working tender first, the locomotive will run chimney first for the canter down the bank. Banking engine drivers were instructed not to take less than 10min from Campden to Honeybourne or 20min returning from Moreton. *J. R. P. Hunt*

Station North, pushed facing point bolt lever 33 into the frame, reversed the facing point 32, rebolting it with 33 before lowering signals 56 and 46. When the brake van was clear of the crossover from down to up branch line, he dismantled the last route and set up the new one — crossover 28 reversed and signal levers 3, 12 and 13 lowered after the East Junction signalman had 'given the road'. The train could then reverse all the way round to East Junction — a distance of about a mile. At the site of the old North Junction, where the Stratford and Cheltenham lines diverged, the gradient changed and the brake van tipped over a brow as the rest of the train came uphill. This was where the guard screwed his hand brake on to prevent the wagons from running on and causing the sort of snatch that might break a coupling. The train stopped when the engine was clear of the

crossover at East Junction and then, when the road was set, drew forwards to the down line for Cheltenham. This was the fine weather procedure. In fog or falling snow the instructions ordered that an engine be coupled to the brake van and that this engine draw the train round to East Junction, the train engine merely trailing along as part of the load or acting as banker if necessary. If for some reason a passenger train had to be reversed — perhaps a troop train or some other special — then a different procedure was laid down. The train ran to the down branch platform, after which the train engine was uncoupled and then reversed to East Junction along the up branch line. At East Junction it was crossed to the down Cheltenham line. The banking engine then backed on to the rear of the passenger train and drew it from down to up branch and round to East Junction where the

train engine backed on to its train and took it away.

Another indication of how busy the work was at Honeybourne are the relaxations of the standard rules. At Honeybourne freight trains could be propelled (ie pushed not pulled) between the Station North and South boxes on either line and in the wrong direction (eg up the down downline) and they could be hauled between those places in the wrong direction providing that in every case the signalman agreed and that, in the case of a propelling movement, a man rode on the leading wagon. If this had been a covered van the man would have ridden on the buffer, a precarious perch. It was also permitted to run a train between the boxes without a brake van provided someone rode on the last wagon with a red light. Obviously all these dispensations were needed to permit the place to work as smoothly and as quickly as possible in between the stopping passenger trains and the expresses. Even so, Oxford footplatemen will tell you that to take a goods down to Honeybourne and back was 'a 12hr job' the yards were so busy.

Honeybourne Bank was the scene of the first, fully authenticated achievement of a speed of 100mph by a Great Western locomotive when, in 1939, 'Castle' 4-6-0 No 4086 *Builth Castle* made that speed at the foot of the incline and through the station. Going up the bank the running was slower but no less exciting for the lineside observer. Passenger trains with an overload for the 3½-mile-long incline would normally come double-headed from Worcester unless they were booked to call at Honeybourne, in which case they could put the banker on ahead of the train engine. Passenger trains were not banked but piloted on

Above:
A view from the bridge looking towards Oxford. From left to right the tracks are, up goods loop, up and down branch, up and down main, down goods loop and down siding.
M. J. Lewis

Campden Bank. In 1936 a 'Castle' was permitted to take a load of 427 tons unassisted, a 'Hall' 392 tons and a '43xx' 2-6-0 364 tons. There was also, of course, the engine's inclination to make steam to be taken into account and a 'rough' engine would have to have assistance with less than the permitted single-engine load for the bank.

Freight trains with an excessive load for the bank were assisted in the rear to Campden or Moreton-in-the-Marsh. In the former case the banker was not coupled to the brake van, but in the latter case it was, owing to the steep falling gradient between Campden and Aston Magna, ¾-mile beyond Blockley (the latter was 2 miles from Campden). From Aston Magna the line rose at 1 in 100/1 in 150 for a mile or so towards Moreton and was on a curve or curves so sharp as to make wheel flanges bind on rails and thus create extra work for the engine. As my mate Charlie Turner told me, 'If you had a rough engine you'd have the banker through to Moreton whether or not you got a run through Blockley because that little bank with those curves at Aston Magna could be a killer'. The maximum load for a '28xx' 2-8-0 from Honeybourne to Moreton, getting a clear run through Blockley, was a massive '60 of coal' in 1936. A 'Hall' 4-6-0 or '43xx' 2-6-0 could take 41 and a pannier tank of the '57xx' variety '31 of coal' according to the official instructions.

A train requiring the banker only as far as Campden, providing it got a clear run through Blockley, was specially signalled from Honeybourne — the Station South signalman sending the code 2-2-3 after South Junction had acknowledged the two beats 'Train Entering Section'. This was relayed on to Campden and the man there made arrangements with Moreton and Blockley. If it turned out that Moreton could not give Blockley

'Line Clear' for the goods then it was stopped at Campden and allowed to wait 10min in the hope that it would 'get the road'. If after all that it still could not be accepted by Moreton, the train driver was told to give the banker 'four crows' on the whistle. The fireman of the banker then coupled his engine to the train, the 'four crows' whistle was acknowledged and the train set off. A small pinch of salt should be taken with these official instructions because the Worcester line signalmen were very jealous of their 'Londons' (the expresses) and the idea of allowing a freight to stand on the main line, waiting, for 10min is therefore a novel one. Oxford footplatemen recall that 'if the fast was an hour behind they'd put you inside out of its way'.

The year 1955 was probably one of the busiest in the history of the station. If the working timetable is to be believed the station and outlying junctions were busier in that year than in 1935. Below is a list of the trains scheduled into or past Honeybourne station in one hour on a summer weekday in 1955. It cannot include seasonal extras, excursions or extra trains for fruit and vegetable traffic nor can it include the shunting trips, light engines dashing to turn on one of the triangular junctions or any of the multitude of other small movements which once contributed to the activities around a busy station or signalbox. This is the basic schedule — supposing all the time that the trains ran to schedule.

Train	Headcode	South Jc	West Jc	East Jc	Station	West Jc	East Jc
3.35am Banbury-Honeybourne	'H'	—	—	7.55	8.00/	—	—
8.00am Honeybourne-S.T. Jc	'H'	—	—	—	/8.00	8.04	—
8.05am Honeybourne-Leamington	'B'	—	—	—	/8.05	—	8.08
1.05am Swindon-Oxley	'F'	8.09	—	8.11/8.20	—	—	—
8.00am Evesham-Birmingham	'B'	—	—	—	8.10/8.11	—	8.14
8.15am Honeybourne-Aldington	'K'	—	—	—	/8.15	—	—
7.15am Great Malvern-Padd	'A'	—	—	—	8.16 n/s	—	—
7.05am Leamington-Honeybourne	'B'	—	—	8.23	8.25/	—	—
7.35am Cheltenham-Evesham	'B'	—	8.32	—	8.36/8.37	—	—
5.45am Banbury-S.T. Jc	'F'	—	—	8.32	—	8.34	—
6.45am Worcester-Kingham	'K'	—	—	—	8.30/9.30	—	—
8.00am Worcester-Birmingham	'B'	—	—	—	8.43/8.46	—	8.48
11.50pm Neath-Honeybourne	'H'	—	—	—	8.50/	—	—
8.20am Worcester-Moreton	'B'	—	—	—	8.56/8.58	—	—

'A' is express train, belled through the signal boxes with 4 beats
'B' is stopping passenger train 3-1 beats
'F' is express freight not fitted with the continuous brake 3-2 beats
'K' is freight stopping at intermediate stations 3 beats
'H' is through freight 1-4 beats

The 8.05am Honeybourne and the 8.20am Worcester were scheduled for diesel railcars.
The 7.35am Cheltenham was an 'auto' train.

Above:
Looking towards Stratford with Honeybourne West Loop
signals lowered for that direction. The left-hand arm signals
the route to the station. The Oxford to Worcester line crosses
on the second bridge under which lies the junction for the
West Curve. March 1975. *R. I. Wallace*

Traffic throughout the 1950s ran in quantities not seen since before World War 1; indeed, passenger and freight traffic forwarded from the station was greater in 1959 than in 1903 or 1913. In 1953, a total of 34,776 ordinary tickets and 650 seasons were sold — a theoretical daily average of 81 passengers. No less than 6,800 tons of general merchandise was forwarded along with 15 wagonloads of cattle. In 1959, 28,942 ordinary tickets and 786 seasons were sold while 3,483 tons of general merchandise were forwarded. No cattle were loaded. The Honeybourne to Cheltenham local service was withdrawn from 7 March 1960 and the Honeybourne to Stratford locals came off on 3 January 1966 leaving two fast trains in each direction between Worcester, Honeybourne and Stratford. These were withdrawn from 6 May 1969 and the entire station was closed and later demolished. The peculiar business whereby a plywood box masquerading as Honeybourne station was given a ceremonial opening on 22 May 1981, three days before any trains stopped there, need not concern us here.

Left:
Honeybourne West Loop signalbox with one siding still connected but only a line of trees to show the line of the other one. June 1975. *R. I. Wallace*

Below:
A very grimy Stanier 'Black Five' 4-6-0, with a confident plume of steam coming off the safety valves, crosses the West Curve Junction points on its way north with the 12.30pm Penzance to Wolverhampton on 14 August 1965. *M. Mensing*

Kemble

Above:
Kemble station from the east end. The old East signalbox is on the left and the Cirencester branch is on the right. A 'gassing' wagon stands against the buffers nearest the camera. The utter neatness of the scene seems to be quite remarkable to our eyes. Note the patiently trimmed yew bushes and the skyline dominated by the village water supply tank. About 1921. *L&GRP*

Kemble station stands precisely at Milepost 91 from Paddington on the line from Swindon to Gloucester. The first railway through this district of rolling farmland, was I. K. Brunel's Swindon to Cirencester line opened on 31 May 1841. It was not really a branch line, more a secondary main line at that time. The greatest obstacle to be overcome in building the route was not geographical but human — in the person of Squire Robert Gordon of Kemble House. He professed an utter detestation of railways and made up his mind that none should pass through his land. He owned a great acreage in the parish of Kemble, indeed, one could say he *was* Kemble. However, the sum of 7,500 gold sovereigns, proffered as 'compensation for damages to be sustained', convinced him that he might be able to live with the railway and he graciously agreed to sell the required land to the Cheltenham & Great Western Union Railway. Even then he placed remarkable conditions on the Company. Neither the railway nor even a plume of steam was to be visible from the windows of his mansion, so a tunnel 415yd long was made where a cutting would have sufficed; no public station was to be built on his land and, for good measure, he made the railway build a road bridge over the Thames somewhere in his parish.

On 12 May 1845 Brunel's line from Milepost 90¾ to Gloucester was opened, thus making the line to Cirencester rather more of a branch line. As Gordon had forbidden any stations on his land, all that could be provided at the point of divergence was a pair of wooden platforms to allow the interchange of passsengers between trains. From a remark made by the Board of Trade's Inspecting Officer, Gen Pasley, there platforms seem to have been placed further east than the site of the present station. Although there was no station as such there must have been a certain number of points in the vicinity to allow through passenger and freight trains to run — as they undoubtedly did — between Swindon and Cirencester, but it is unlikely that there was a direct facing connection to the branch line.

A proper station for passengers and goods was built immediately west of the Tetbury to Cirencester Road, the Fosse Way. The road marked the boundary of Gordon's land and the new station was built where it passed under the railway embankment, between Mileposts 91¾ and 92 from Paddington. It was situated three miles along the dead straight road from Cirencester and seven miles from Tetbury so it was named 'Tetbury

Left:
Kemble station from the down platform, east end, looking along the Cirencester branch. The small cabin at the far end of the branch platform housed the electric train staff instrument for the branch. Someone is still taking care of the yew bushes. The photograph was taken in about 1933. *L&GRP*

Below left:
The Cirencester branch platform looking towards the main line with the booking and other offices in the fine stone building to the right. A 1905-vintage shed, with a 'pagoda' roof is acting as a lock-up for bicycles or parcels destined for branch trains. The shed is made of Taylor of Birmingham's patent 'Universal roof covering and building material'. *M. Hale*

Right:
A view of Kemble looking west in 1963 with a trimmed-down signalling system and some untrimmed yew bushes. Whose retirement is responsible for their unkempt state after three generations? The little 'jockey' tank still rides bravely on the main tank at the far end of the station. *M. J. Lewis*

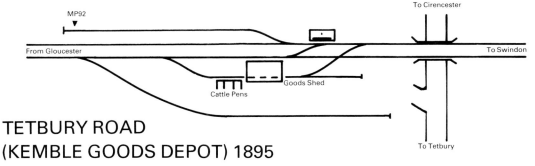

TETBURY ROAD
(KEMBLE GOODS DEPOT) 1895

Road' so as not to take traffic off the Cirencester branch railway. The new structure is believed to have resembled Brimscombe (the next station down the line), having low, stone buildings and a wide canopy reaching out on all four sides. There was also a large, dressed stone goods shed to cater for the imports and exports of a widely scattered agricultural community — a large proportion of which presumably came from the Gordon estate.

Tetbury Road remained the station for passengers and freight until 30 April 1882 when it was closed to passengers — a full 10 years after the present Kemble station had been opened on Miss Anna Gordon's land. The old station must have been very useful, being on the main road between towns, in spite of its apparent remote-

ness. During the narrowing of the gauge of the Cirencester branch on 22-27 May 1872, passengers were conveyed by horse and carriage from Cirencester to Tetbury Road — the latter being easier to reach than the freshly opened Kemble station.

The change of heart at the 'Big House' was gratefully recognised by the GWR by the erection of a truly splendid station. It was built of a smooth, white stone with the obligatory pointed gables and massive chimneys, yet in a single-storey style so that it was relatively unobtrusive — a most obsequious station as was right and proper. Imaginative use was made of glass and wood to provide plenty of light and shelter. Furthermore, by taking advantage of the 'V'-shaped site between

Above:
Kemble station seen from the down side approach road in 1964 with evidence of a healthy passenger traffic. The platform for the now closed Tetbury branch is on the left, that for the Cirencester branch on the right. *M. J. Lewis*

the two routes, the architect created a handsome, triangular concourse between the booking offices and those on the platform side, sheltering it at the side and top with his glass screens. In later years some fine topiary developed on the platforms and, coming on the station from the slope above, one looked down on what might have been a country house with a railway running through it. At such a discreet place there could be no inwards or outwards freight service — nothing which smacked of 'Trade' — and throughout its history Kemble never had a goods department — all that was handled up at Tetbury Road until the latter was finally closed on 1 July 1963.

In 1865 the Cirencester branch, not quite 5¼ miles long, was worked by the Train Staff and Ticket system with a policeman to walk the layout and operate the points and signals. Four down goods trains and at least as many on the up line called at the Kemble interchange to detach and pick up traffic to and from the Cirencester branch and these also called to work at Tetbury Road. Swindon to Gloucester passenger trains connected with branch trains at the Kemble platforms, calling afterwards at Tetbury Road. One train in each direction, the 8.10pm Paddington to New Milford and the 5.10pm from New Milford, both Mail trains, ignored the platforms and stopped at Tetbury Road. Being hard by the Fosse Way this station was far more convenient for the carriage of mails to Tetbury and Cirencester when the alternative required travel over the badly maintained parish roads around Kemble. In 1875 there were at least 19 passenger trains and 16 goods trains calling at or passing through Kemble and Tetbury Road, including the aforesaid Mail trains and a newcomer. The latter was the 6.10am Brimscombe light engine which came over Sapperton Bank to Tetbury Road, collected empty coaches there and brought them on to Kemble. There, the locomotive ran round the stock which then formed the 8.25am to Gloucester. It is possible that by this year or shortly afterwards a signalbox was erected on the down side at the east end of the station. It was in operation by 1884.

The 7¼-mile-long branch line from the west end of Kemble station to Tetbury was built by the Great Western Railway — rather unusually as such lines were normally the work of a local company — and opened on 2 December 1889. It seems reasonable to suppose that the Kemble West signalbox was built to operate the small extra layout required by the additional branch line. At any rate, there were two signalboxes working the station until 1929. In spite of the existence of a long, single track branch, worked by the electric Train Staff and Block Telegraph system, the old station at Tetbury Road continued to fulfil a role. In 1903, traffic at both Kemble and Tetbury Road was holding up well as the figures below suggest:

Kemble*

Staff	Paybill £	Income £	Tickets	General merchandise Fwd (tons)	Rec (tons)	Cattle fwd
14†	872†	3,323	19,089	—	—	—

* No goods traffic dealt with here. (GWR Traffic Statistics. PRO Rail 266/46.)
† Includes four men working at Tetbury Road.

Tetbury Road

Staff	Paybill £	Income £	Tickets	General merchandise Fwd (tons)	Rec (tons)	Cattle fwd
—	—	1,559	—	1,414	1,428	43

Above:
The up platform and passageway to the booking office and Cirencester branch platform in 1964.
M. J. Lewis

Left:
A view inside the passageway or concourse showing how well the station was designed. It is sheltered, well lit and, above all, dignified with a sense of fine design and construction. The Cirencester platform is at the far end.
Reg Farrell/Author's Collection

One of the specialities or features of Kemble in the last quarter of the 19th century were the water trains. Trains of tanks and converted locomotive tenders were brought there to be filled with water for locomotive, industrial and domestic purposes in Swindon shed and locomotive works, the Swindon local supply being insufficient to meet demand. Water tanks also came from wayside stations, in those days long before the provision of piped water supplies, to be filled at the Kemble well. In 1902 a great expansion of Swindon Works was planned so work was begun to ensure a greatly increased output of water from Kemble. The station is about one mile from the source of the River Thames and is well provided with pure water. A fine pumping house was built in the 'V' of the junction between the Tetbury branch and the main line and inside were placed two hand-fired Lancashire boilers and two, two-cylinder compound engines side by side. They had high pressure cylinders 18in in diameter and low pressure cylinders 32in in diameter with a 24in stroke. Turning at a majestic 12rpm, one engine worked to raise water from 35ft below ground to the big tank at the platform end, 22ft above the rails. The other engine was on stand-by. From the main tank, water flowed the 13 miles to Swindon through a 15in diameter pipeline laid in a trench alongside the down main line. The great fear was always that, should the pipeline burst, the water would wash away the trackbed from beneath the track, especially if the burst occurred on an embankment. Fortunately this was a very rare event, if indeed it ever happened at all. Contingency plans were laid of course. Alarm bells linked to a pressure gauge showing the pressure in

the pipeline were fitted in one of the Kemble signalboxes so that the signalman would know, should the alarm bell ring, if this was a false alarm — there being no reduction of pressure in the pipe — or a true emergency. In the latter case he was instructed to send the 'Obstruction Danger' signal to Minety and telephone the signalman there with the reason why the bell had been sent. The emergency code would then be sent through all the boxes back to and including Swindon Locomotive Yard box and the line would be closed until it had been examined by competent men riding on an engine. The 1945 instructions also laid down that the engine was to push a shunter's trolley before it and the men were to go equipped with a portable telephone. A plug-in socket had been provided on the telegraph post nearest to each quarter milepost so that, on locating the burst, a message could instantly be sent, by telephone, to the nearest signalbox.

Around 1933 the steam pumps at Kemble were superseded by electric motors but the older machines were kept in perfect working order in case of the failure of the electricity supply. On the first Thursday of each month, at 11.05am a '57xx' 0-6-0PT, preferably one fresh out of shops, was sent from Swindon to Kemble to steam the pumps. Apparently, this was a job that took all that a large pannier tank with a boiler pressure of 200lb/sq in could give.

By 1908 Kemble was enjoying a first-rate passenger service both by day and by night and by that time a pattern was set that was to last through to the Beeching era — in fact, the 'small hours' call of a London express lasted after the branches had been shut. The 9.15pm Paddington-Neyland Mail

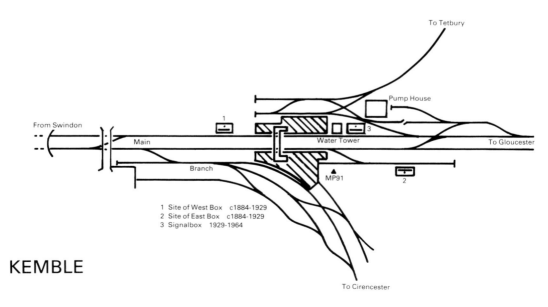

1 Site of West Box   c1884-1929
2 Site of East Box   c1884-1929
3 Signalbox   1929-1964

KEMBLE

At the west end of the station '57XX' 0-6-0PT No 4651 runs round its train in the summer of 1964. The line falls downhill towards the down main advanced starter signal but rises from there to the summit at Sapperton. Kemble signalbox was one of the most highly polished the author ever visited. *Author*

Right:
The driver of '57XX' 0-6-0PT No 4651 looks out carefully as he eases his engine up to its coach on the up main line at Kemble in the summer of 1964. The view along the upside approach road gives some idea of the handsome Cotswold surroundings of the station. *Author*

Left:
Inside the pump house at Kemble. Even here, at the very end of their lives, these magnificent engines look as good as new with not a spot of oil anywhere except on the moving surfaces. Freddie Boots, the man from Swindon Works who came down to make regular checks on the electric pumps, made sure the steam engines were clean although it was no part of his job so to do. He had a great loyalty to the job. *Author*

called at 11.41pm and the 1am Paddington-West Wales express called at 3.15am with no connection to either branch. Including the 5.42am Paddington, which called at Kemble at 8.15am and the 1pm Neyland-Paddington stopping train at 9.05pm, 10 down and 11 up passenger trains serviced the station. Of these, three in each direction were 'A' class expresses calling most conveniently at mid-morning, lunch-time and tea-time.

Three up and three down pick-up goods trains called to shunt — the 1.05am Gloucester from 2.30am until 3am, just as the 8.10pm Didcot arrived to shunt until 4.10am — all of which must have been very nice for the people sleeping in the cottages on the bank just above the shunting yard. Six main line goods trains were scheduled to take water at Kemble. The branch line trains were well timed to meet the frequent main line trains, although the shorter Cirencester branch was better able to make connections than the Tetbury line which, being nearly twice as long as the Cirencester and having intermediate halts along the way had a journey time of 17min against 8min on the Cirencester branch. The engine on the latter was a real 'dasher' making 14 round trips per day with passenger trains and two more, its first and last journeys, with freight. There were six round trips on the longer, Tetbury line. Some of the trips on both lines were worked as mixed trains with freight vehicles attached behind the passenger carriages. The Cirencester branch could boast four 'station trucks' which were detached from early morning freights and worked back to the junction on the 4.12pm. Each truck was branded with a number and its set route: No 470 worked between Birkenhead and Cirencester, No 471 to and from Manchester, No 473 to Hockley (Birmingham) and No 474 to Cardiff daily. What the timetable does not state is what they were carrying.

The Tetbury trains could not connect with every main line working but the Cirencester trains could and did. However, both the branches provided a good service and examples of how connections were made are given below:

	C'ctr	T'by	Swindon 'B'	Cardiff 'B'		Cardiff 'A'	
	9.20	9.16	9.13am	6.30am		7.55am	
Kemble arr	9.28	9.33	9.39	9.50		10.22	
dep			9.41	9.55	10.05	10.24	10.32
					10.36		10.40
					T'by		C'ctr

	C'ctr	T'by	Chelt' 'A'	C'ctr	Pad'ton 'A'		
	12.10	Noon	11.00am	12.47	10.50am		
Kemble arr	12.18	12.21	12.28	12.55	12.56		
dep			12.34	12.34	1.01	1.08	1.12
				12.42		1.28	1.20
				C'ctr		T'by	C'ctr

Right:
Looking across the pump house from one engine to the other. The herringbone gear wheels were engaged by a similar, small-diameter wheel driven by the engine. The large wheel turned and drove a crank to which was attached a horizontal beam constructed of wood sandwiched between steel plate. The reciprocating motion of the horizontal beam went to another crank to which was attached the vertical pumping rod. The cylinder in sight is the low pressure, 32in vessel. The author was told that the pump house was knocked down with the engines still inside and earth spread over the site between the two embankments. It is to be hoped that this is not true. *Author*

In 1908 both branch lines were operated with the Webb-Thompson large electric train staff, the Tetbury line from West box and the Cirencester line from East box. During 1929 these two boxes were abolished and a single, new 62-lever signalbox was opened a few yards beyond the down main platform at the west end. In 1936 the Tetbury line was worked by the system of train staff and only one engine in steam on the line while the Cirencester line continued to be worked with the electric staff although not quite in the usual way. The Tetbury line had six round trips a day in 1936 and passed just behind the signalbox, so that it was easy enough for the Kemble signalman to deliver the train staff to, and retrieve it from, the driver of the train. However, there were 11 passenger trains each way on the Cirencester branch plus three freight trains and he could not be expected to run his signalbox and walk all the way from there to the engine of the branch train perhaps 200yd away on the far side of the station. The arrangement was therefore made that a small cabin housing an electric staff instrument and a 10-lever ground frame was installed at the Cirencester end of the branch platform while in the

signalbox there was a bell in communication with Cirencester box and an indicator working with the electric train staff. A porter or other responsible person would ask the Kemble signalman for a staff and he would ring the bell to 'ask the road' to Cirencester. In replying to this the Cirencester man held down on his morse key at the last stroke and the indicator in Kemble box flicked over. The signalman could then tell the porter to take a staff out as the instrument was electrically unlocked. Should the train have been accepted by Cirencester under the 3-5-5 bell code — the 'Warning Arrangement' indicating that the line ahead of the home signal at Cirencester was occupied — then the Kemble signalman would tell the man operating the staff instrument so that he could instruct the train driver. Because of the somewhat curious geography of the station and the sharp curve on which the Cirencester branch lay, it was not possible for the points at the Cirencester end of the branch platform to be operated by the Kemble signalman, for he could not have watched the movements to know when to alter the points. It was for this reason that the 10-lever frame was provided, worked by a porter. Before the porter could operate any of these levers he had to obtain the signalman's consent and this was given by the reversing of either lever 42 or 43. These were interlocking levers which released the locks on the required levers at the ground frame and locked other levers which it would then have been incorrect to operate.

In 1936 the station was scheduled to receive 17 down passenger trains including seven 'A' class expresses. On the up main there were 15 passenger trains booked to call, of which six were expresses. One of them, the 2.40pm from Cheltenham, was due to leave Swindon at 3.45pm and run non-stop to Paddington, a distance of 77¼ miles, in 65min. This was known to all and sundry as the 'Cheltenham Flyer' although it really only 'flew' between Swindon and London. The 3.15pm Cirencester connected into this train but there was no connection to or from the Tetbury line. The latter still had six round trips a day as it had in 1908 but the Cirencester line was reduced from 14 to 11 passenger round trips per day. In 1936 there were two stopping trains from Swindon to Kemble and back and a lunch-time train from Swindon to Cirencester which returned at tea-time. Some of the Great Western's best express trains called at Kemble in sufficient numbers to provide an excellent service on their own, but this was augmented by a lavish local service offering connections, via Swindon and Gloucester with just about anywhere in the country. In all 60-65 trains a day passed or called at the station on the main line. The station thrived, as can be seen from the figures provided below.

	Staff	Paybill £	Income £	Tickets
1913	15 (4)*	1,014	5,077	21,846
1923	18 (4)*	3,229	6,729	21,643 (62)
1929	18 (3)*	2,433	9,465	26,507 (85)
1930	18 (3)*	2,683	10,828	27,904 (105)
1933	15 (3)*	2,715	9.262	26,195 (123)
1938	16 (2)*	3,719	13,537	33,850 (47)

All goods traffic was dealt with at Kemble.
* The figures in brackets are the numbers of men employed at Coates which were included in the Kemble paybill.

Coates

	Income £	General merchandise Fwd (tons)	Rec (tons)	Cattle fwd
1913	1,543	1,679	1,840	61
1923	2,618	706	1,782	91
1929	1,651	445	1,011	80
1930	1,597	323	650	89
1933	1,652	960	421	69
1938	21,552	1,322	5,011	48

After the war there were more main line trains booked to pass Kemble than ever before. In the summer of 1954, 75 trains of all kinds passed or called at the station each day. On the branch lines matters were very much as they had been since 1908. The Tetbury line still had its six trains each way daily but the Cirencester branch had suffered yet another reduction to nine passenger trains and one freight each way. The three trains each way between Swindon and Kemble also ran but none of them went through to Cirencester. The service was still lavish and all the main line trains connected with the Cirencester branch. Four crack main line expresses each way, including the up and down 'Cheltenham Spa Express' (which was fast but not in any way like the famous 'Cheltenham Flyer') called and connected with the Cirencester trains, but the Tetbury line was not always able to make these particular connections. Thus, on the eve of what might be called 'the Coming of the Motor Car' Kemble and Coates were still fulfilling the role they had played for nearly 100 years.

The Tetbury branch was first to go, closed on 6 May 1964 after various efforts to run it economically had failed, including the use of a lightweight diesel railbus. In passing it must be noted that the GWR does not appear to have used its diesel railcars on either branch line. They remained the preserve of small tank locomotives of the 0-4-2 and 0-6-0 wheel arrangement until the railbus arrived in about 1963. The Cirencester line succumbed on 4 October 1965 but Kemble station continues to provide a service of trains for the people of the area.

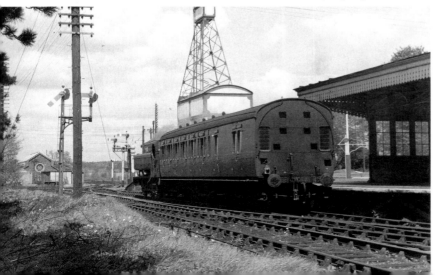

Left:
The signal is lowered for '16XX' 0-6-0PT No 1658 to take the single-coach, 1.10pm Kemble to Tetbury service away on 7 May 1955. The gable of the pump house can be seen between the embankments of the two lines. *R. E. Toop*

Kidlington

Kidlington station began life as Langford Lane on 2 September 1850 but was renamed Woodstock Road later on. The station lay slightly north of Milepost 69 from Paddington, 5½ miles north of Oxford on the line to Banbury. The route was opened in September 1850 as a broad gauge, single track terminating at Banbury but on 1 October 1852 the line was, in a sense, reopened, as a double track, mixed gauge railway from Oxford to Birmingham Snow Hill. Woodstock Road station was built on the south side of the Oxford to Banbury road, close to the Oxford canal, surrounded by a vast expanse of green fields. The hamlet of Kidlington was a mile away to the east and the little town of Woodstock three miles away to the northwest. The station's office was on the down platform and was a single-storey, stone building which had a large bay window at the south end from which passengers could watch out for the approach of their train. A wide canopy, supported on horizontal beams laid across the walls, protruded on all four sides equally and above this was a low, ridged roof with hipped gables. Where the beams slotted into the canopy's outer valance the joint was concealed behind a plaque of wood to which was fixed the stylised representation in cast iron of a lion's head surmouted by a crown. Further north on the Banbury line Heyford and Aynho were also given this type of station and numerous others were built to this design between

Gloucester and Milford Haven, many or all of them carrying the lion's head decoration. In the tiny goods yard there was a simple, stone goods shed, the arches over the road and rail access being formed of timber planking.

The early train service was rudimentary, the service of 1865 and 1875 being practically identical — four slow passenger trains calling in each direction and three freights, two down and one up. In 1875 the spartan layout was operated by a policeman walking the tracks to alter points and turn the disc and cross-bar signals but between 1882 and 1884 a signalbox was erected. The station became a junction on 19 May 1890 when the 3¾-mile-long, single track, standard gauge branch was opened to Woodstock. The station at the far end of the line was close to the town centre and also to the main gate of the Duke of Marlborough's palace at Blenheim. The station began life as Woodstock but became Blenheim & Woodstock later. With the opening of the branch Woodstock

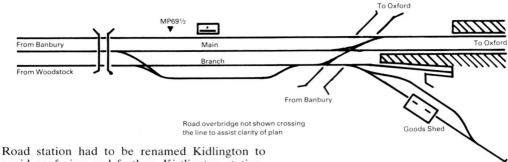

MP69½

From Banbury
Main
To Oxford

From Woodstock
Branch

From Banbury

To Oxford

Road overbridge not shown crossing
the line to assist clarity of plan

Goods Shed

Road station had to be renamed Kidlington to avoid confusion and further, Kirtlington station, two miles down the line had to be renamed Bletchington for the same reason.

The branch brought an enlarged layout and a new signalbox which was sited on the upside of the line about 200yd north of the main road overbridge. The box measured 31ft 9in×11ft 6in with its floor raised 8ft above the rails and was to the then new, standard, GWR signalbox design. There was a 51-lever frame consisting of 28 signal levers, seven points, three facing point bolts and 13 spares. There were originally six round trips a day over the branch which was regulated by the Train Staff and Ticket system to guard against head-on collisions on the single track. The branch engine hauled freight wagons behind the passenger coach or coaches as a mixed train and, once a day, having left the passenger train at Woodstock came back to Kidlington with the freight brake van to work a goods train to the terminus. The system varied little over the years. The line was usually worked by an 0-4-2T and in particular by the '517' class 0-4-2T No 1473 *Fair Rosamund* which was named for the day in 1896 when it hauled a Royal Train from Kidlington to Woodstock. This privilege of carrying a name was unique among the scores of

KIDLINGTON 1891-1906

'517' class engines and No 1473 retained its name until its withdrawal, still working on the branch, in 1935. The name plate is rumoured to have been taken into protective custody within the Woodstock area.

In 1900 traffic on the main line through Kidlington was increasing although the branch service remained steady at six return workings a day. An up refuge siding was provided in that year, extending from the signalbox northwards to the bridge carrying a farm track over the line. This siding, into which a goods train could be backed to allow a following faster train to pass, would have been sorely needed. Between July 1901 and July 1902 the wooden train staff was replaced with the electric staff patented by Webb and Thompson of the LNWR but there was no increase in the branch train service as a result. In 1903 Kidlington station was moderately busy with an average of 39 people a day catching a train there and the total income being nearly seven times greater than the wage bill as shown below.

Staff	Paybill £	Income £	Tickets	General merchandise Fwd (tons)	Rec (tons)	Cattle fwd
9	446	3,010	14,480	1,951	1,248	47

Left:
The view towards Woodstock and Banbury with the road set and signal lowered for the Woodstock branch. Both the arms on the main line signal bracket are of the 3ft variety reserved normally for non-passenger carrying lines. On the left is the signal bracket which starts trains from the branch platform. This carries a 4ft and a 3ft arm according to normal usage.
W. L. Kenning/Author's Collection

Left:
On the Woodstock branch about 700yd north of Kidlington station, looking towards Banbury and Woodstock. The signal for the Woodstock direction is lowered — just — and there is a curious little arm to route trains through the power operated points to the down main line. In the distance can be seen the up branch outer home giving a clearing point for a down train in the loop.
W. L. Kenning/Author's Collection

Below:
After the Woodstock branch had closed W. L. Kenning took this view of Signalman Edgar Walton at the power points. In the distance is the station.
W. L. Kenning/Author's Collection

Above:
On the last day of trains on the Woodstock branch the auto-train coasts downhill towards the main line. The driver, Arthur Hall, is driving from the leading end of the coach. The main line can be seen below the left-hand buffer of the locomotive. *P. G. Barlow/Author's Collection*

There was no refuge siding on the down side but it was possible to place a down freight train into the branch provided that the train was not too long. The down branch to main points were 166yd from the box which was nearly the maximum distance permitted under the Board of Trade's regulations as they existed in 1890. A down goods train was reversed through the crossover in the station to the up main and it could then run forward into the loop or branch line. It was normal practice to place a down train on to the up line in order to allow a following train to pass so it was no hardship, in the context of times, to do this movement in order to get a train into a goods loop. Such a manoeuvre blocking the single track branch had to be protected from collision. What system was originally used is unclear, but from 1906 stringent and complicated measures were adopted. First the effective length of the branch-cum-loop and the shorter loop to the west of this was increased, due

doubtless to a relaxation of the Board of Trade's regulations on the length of rodding to facing points. The shortest loop was extended by about 35yd and the points from down branch to down main were taken up and resited 70ft north of the farm track bridge. At the south or station end of the loop a facing point was laid from the down main to the branch, while the connection from the crossover to the branch was retained. These two points had to be inoperable unless the electric train staff was in the control instrument and, when a train was occupying the loop, it had to be impossible to withdraw a staff from either end of the Kidlington-Woodstock section.

If the signalman at Kidlington wanted to put a down goods train into the loop he could if he had not permitted the Woodstock signalman to withdraw a staff for a train to proceed. The Kidlington man sent the bell code 5-2 to Woodstock and the man there repeated this, holding down his morse key on the final beat. The Kidlington man held down on his morse key and at the same time turned and removed an Annett's key from its lock. The action of removing this 6in-long brass key from its electrically locked instrument had the effect of breaking the circuit to the staff instrument. The small key was then inserted into the mechanical lock fitted to the lever which worked the bolt of the facing point into the

down loop-cum-branch. When pushed into the lock the key projected by no more than an inch or two and thus did not form an obstruction to the signalman as he moved about his levers as would have been the case if a 2ft-long Webb-Thompson staff had been used to unlock the lever — a system which was used in less confined spaces. Turning the Annett's key in the lever's lock allowed the lever to be reversed, withdrawing the bolt in the facing points and freeing the interlocking on the lever working the facing point blades.

The years before World War 1 were a period of peace and stability for the Woodstock branch and Kidlington station. Apart from the days when No 1473 was away for a boiler wash-out or repairs, the little engine shuttled to and fro, being worked by the same driver, fireman and guard and being supervised by the same stationmaster year in, year out. Kidlington's stationmaster, William Thomas Cook came to the station as a booking porter in May 1890 and retired from there as stationmaster in 1927 with 51 years of service to the Great Western. The train services remained virtually unchanged for years. In 1908 there were eight round trips on the branch each day with a provisional path for a (fairly regular) excursion from Oxford to Blenheim Palace and also a late night Saturdays Only return trip from Oxford for the benefit of those visiting the pubs and theatres.

At this time the through workings were handled by a steam railmotor. There was one in each direction during the week — from Oxford to Woodstock leaving Kidlington at 2.09pm and returning from Woodstock at 2.52pm and leaving Kidlington at 4pm on a through trip to Princes Risborough via Thame. On the main line, 25 goods trains were scheduled to pass Kidlington — most of them at night — and among these were the two or three which called to pick up and set down wagons. Prior to World War 1, the summer timetables around the 1905 to 1914 period, were increasingly filled with express trains as the railway woke up and was equipped with really powerful engines. Among them were expresses from Great Central territory, from Sheffield and beyond and from Newcastle and York, which came up through Kidlington behind Great Central Atlantics in their dark green, brass and Indian red finery. The engines usually came off at Oxford but the coaches went through to Dover and Plymouth. During the day the Kidlington signalman would have had the pleasure of pulling off not only for *Fair Rosamund* and the steam railmotor but also for Dean 'Singles' and

Robinson's 'Jersey Lilies'. He must have done a fair amount of lever pulling because in 1918 his 1890 vintage, double-twist frame was replaced with a new, horizontal tappet machine of the latest design.

After World War 1 and, more particularly, after the General Strike of 1926 the travelling public (an increasingly large body of people) discovered the door-to-door convenience (but not comfort) of the road motorcoach for long and short journeys. Special bus services and even lorry services, put on especially to cover the work normally done by the local rail network during the strike were so much appreciated that they remained in force and shortly became properly organised into a real bus service. The railwaymen had let road transport 'get a foot in the door' and the door was to be forced open ever wider. Early in 1928 the signalbox at Woodstock was abolished and the 'auto-train' system of working with the wooden train staff was instituted. The 'auto' or 'push-pull' train was permitted to run without a guard so both the signalman's and guard's wages were saved together with the costs of maintenance of the Woodstock

box and its equipment. There was no longer an electric staff to be locked into its instrument so the down goods loop had to find another form of protection. Trains left Woodstock at their booked time without reference to the Kidlington signalman so an outer home signal was provided against up branch trains, this signal being placed 600yd on the approach side of the down loop to down main points and thus providing an ample 'clearing point' for a train standing in the loop, waiting to 'go out main line'. In May 1942 the loop to main points were resited 679yd further north so that the loop could accommodate several trains. The points were then worked by an electric motor, the current coming from a hand generator in the signalbox.

Three years before the General Strike, ticket sales at Kidlington were three times greater than three years after the strike. A small part of this fall was due to the general depression of trade and employment in that year, but even in 1938 passenger journeys from the station were only half what they had been 15 years earlier. The table below tells the tale.

	Staff	Paybill £	Income £	Tickets	General merchandise (tons)		
					Fwd	Rec	Cattle fwd
1913	10	507	2,921	16,537	1,476	861	119
1923	10	1,438	4,461	13,423 (88)	1,311	1,369	104
1929	10	1,335	4,969	6,533 (27)	434	1,459	88
1930	10	1,289	3,592	6,656 (30)	563	1,052	112
1933	10	1,284	2,593	6,880 (10)	264	830	88
1938	10	1,593	3,821	7,567 (20)	438	1,279	131

Below left:
Collett '14XX' 0-4-2T No 1420 leaves Kidlington with a mixed train for Woodstock. The signal routes trains to the bay, left-hand arm or out on to the up main. Below the latter arm is a calling-on arm erected in May 1942. This view was taken shortly before the closure of the branch.
P. G. Barlow/Author's Collection

Above:
Kidlington in more prosperous days. The legendary '517' Class 0-4-2T No 1473 *Fair Rosamund* poses with her driver Bert Pomeroy, Fireman Ted Harmon and Stationmaster William Cook. The engine has only just run round its train and staff have not yet carried the side and tail lamps to the opposite end of the carriage. The date is 5 February 1921.
W. L. Kenning/Author's Collection

But if Kidlington followed the pattern of other stations, traffic after World War 2 and well into the 1950s was as brisk as it had been before 1914, if measured in terms of tickets sold. Unfortunately the later statistics for Kidlington were unobtainable. The last service on the branch line was eight trips a day with two trips from Woodstock to Oxford and back, all worked by the usual '14xx' 0-4-2T with mixed trains being the norm on the branch. The branch passenger and goods service was withdrawn on and from 1 March 1954, but the station remained in use for passengers on main line trains until 2 November 1964. A goods service was maintained until 1 March 1965. The signalbox and the down goods loop — the last remaining vestiges of the branch line — were taken out of use on 16 September 1968.

KIDLINGTON 1906-54

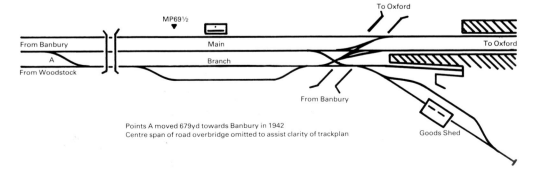

Points A moved 679yd towards Banbury in 1942
Centre span of road overbridge omitted to assist clarity of trackplan

Above:
The Kidlington signalman snatches the wooden Train Staff from the driver's hand as the branch train canters up the home straight towards the bay platform.
P. G. Barlow/Author's Collection

Below:
About 40 years later, shortly before withdrawal of the remaining main line trains, Kidlington station stands shabby and unwanted. The twice-daily traffic jams from Kidlington to Oxford have so far been unsuccessful in bringing about the reinstatement of a railhead here. *Lens of Sutton*

Kingham

Kingham station began life as Chipping Norton Junction and lay about 17 miles southeast of Honeybourne and 21¼ miles northwest of Oxford, on the main line of the Oxford, Worcester & Wolverhampton Railway (OWWR). The station was opened on 10 August 1855 as the main line end of the 4½-mile, single track branch to the cloth manufacturing town of Chipping Norton. The branch ran roughly northeast from the junction and climbed to its terminus on gradients of 1 in 95 or steeper. There was never a facing connection from the branch to the main line but branch trains ran to their own platform reaching the up main line through a trailing connection. The junction station and branch came under the rule of the West Midland Railway (WMR) from 1 July 1860 when the OWWR, the Newport, Abergavenny & Hereford and Worcester & Hereford Railways amalgamated. On 1 March 1862 the WMR opened its 6½-mile, single track branch from Chipping Norton Junction to the market town of Bourton-on-the-Water, passing around the foot of the great hill on which stood Stow on the Wold. The single track curved through the fields on 1 in 80 gradients with never a thought for speed or future developments. At the junction the layout was curious after the manner of the day, the fear of facing points, and must have been difficult to work; the policemen must have walked miles during their 12hr shifts as they altered the widely

Above:
The view of the down side offices at Kingham in 1964. The 1850 vintage buildings looked good for another 100 years but British Rail demolished them. *M. J. Lewis*

dispersed points to manoeuvre the incoming and outgoing trains and to shunt the several goods trains that called to pick up and cut off wagons.

Both branch lines were worked by the Train Staff and Ticket system while the main line was operated under the Time Interval system. If there were two trains to go down a branch line then the first took a ticket and the second brought the staff and only when the staff had arrived at the far end could a train leave that end under the authority of a ticket or the staff. The Bourton branch staff was a cylindrically shaped piece of wood with a brass plate bearing the name of the section to which it applied, while the card tickets were circular and pink. On the Chipping Norton branch the staff was green and square in section while the ticket was also green and square. In 1875 Chipping Norton branch trains were booked to take 15min for the downhill 4½-mile run to the junction and 20min for the outward journey uphill. The somewhat pedestrian schedule was due to the need to haul freight vehicles behind the passenger coaches uphill and the need for extreme caution in descending the hill with only the most rudimentary

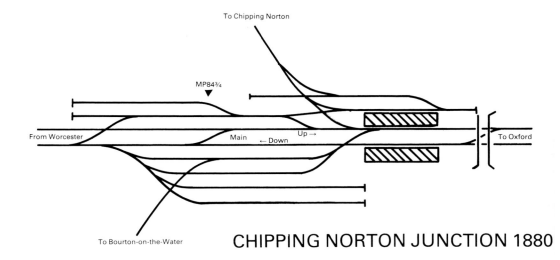

To Chipping Norton

MP84¾ ▼

From Worcester

Main ← Down Up →

To Oxford

To Bourton-on-the-Water

CHIPPING NORTON JUNCTION 1880

of brakes. The schedule was slow, so drivers did not have to hurry.

Chipping Norton line trains connected with all main line passenger services, but the Bourton branch train arrived too late for the first down main line passenger although it met all the rest through the day. In the course of 24hr in 1875, 23 main line passenger trains called at or passed through Chipping Norton Junction; while there were seven arrivals and departures on the Chipping Norton line and five more in each

direction from Bourton. Each branch train's engine had to run round its carriages in order to return whence it came and had also to marshall freight wagons to the rear; the Bourton line trains had the additional shunting involved in getting from the up main platform back to the branch as a glance at Fig 1 will show. There were also 12 main line goods trains which called to shunt although most of this took place at night. The busiest period for freight shunting at the junction was from 9.20pm to midnight as indicated below.

Below:
Kingham station around 1930 looking south along the up main platform. The nameboard announces KINGHAM change for CHIPPING NORTON, BOURTON on the WATER, BANBURY & CHELTENHAM LINES. *P. A. Hopkins*

Working	*Period of shunt*
7.25pm Oxford	9.20-9.30pm
4.05pm Wolverhampton	10.55-11.05pm
8.00pm Didcot	11.00-11.15pm
10.20pm Oxford	11.55-midnight

Top:
Looking north along the up main platform about 1930. A beautifully groomed, perfectly maintained station which, in 1930, carried an average of three passengers in 2hr each day through the year. *P. A. Hopkins*

Above:
Looking south along the Cheltenham arrival platform about 1930. The signal bracket on the left-hand, Chipping Norton arrival platform controls the routes to Banbury with the left-hand arm with Kingham East's fixed distant below, the centre arm routes trains to the down main line, while the right-hand arm controls access to the Cheltenham line. The signal applies to movements from the platform in the foreground and is placed to the right of such trains so as to be easily visible to drivers of right-hand drive, GWR locomotives. *P. A. Hopkins*

All this shunting was done in darkness, and the trains ran through the night on the very shaky principle of a time interval between them with the most rudimentary of signalling and brakes. The despatch of trains from Chipping Norton Junction, the responsibility of warning the drivers about the state of the line and the alteration of each set of points individually by walking over the ballast to the ground lever was the work of the policeman. Perhaps there were two at Chipping Norton Junction, a 'North' beat and a 'South' beat. Signalling at the station was sparse with home signals on up and down main lines and on each branch plus auxiliary or distant signals which were probably worked by lever and wire as a concession to the policeman's legs. There was no interlocking between the signals and points and safety at the junction depended entirely on the physical fitness of the policeman or men.

On 1 June 1881 the Banbury & Cheltenham Direct Railway (B&CDR) opened a 16½-mile extension of the Bourton branch from an end-on junction at Bourton to a new junction called Landsdown about a mile south of Cheltenham St James station. Westwards from Bourton the line fell and rose at 1 in 60 and 1 in 80 until it reached Notgrove summit, whence it plunged towards the River Severn down a 2-mile, 1 in 60 incline to Andoversford — but even then the descent was less than half complete. Anything less like a 'Direct' railway for express passenger trains could not be imagined. Indeed, so steep were the grades that they restricted the use of the line for heavy freight owing to the need for double heading and double brake van provision.

The 1879 survey of Chipping Norton Junction shows the absence of a turntable — the two short branch lines could easily be worked by tank engines so a turntable was not needed but the 1884 survey shows that a table had been installed. This must have been in connection with the extension to Cheltenham some 23 miles away and the anticipated use of tender engines.

On 24 November 1884 the Board of Trade's Inspecting Officer approved the reconstruction of Chipping Norton Junction. A new station was built with longer platforms. Originally these had been about 363ft long; the new ones, extending north and south of the old, were about 534ft (the down main platform) and 478ft (the up main) long. The up Chipping Norton branch platform, the most easterly of the three, was not altered and thus marked the 1855 position of the station. Proper signalling was installed at this time with North and South signalboxes on the up side of the line. The North box was 110yd north of Milepost 84¾ while the South box, squeezed in between the foot of the up platform ramp and the road bridge, was 132yd south of that milepost.

On 1 June 1887, the B&CDR opened a single track railway from King's Sutton Junction, 3½ miles south of Banbury on the line to Oxford, to a new through station at Chipping Norton, linking into the original branch line a short distance to the west of the original terminus, which then became a goods depot. Hilly and serpentine though the

Left:
'Large Prairie' 2-6-2T No 4160 reverses on to its train having run round. Later it will leave Cheltenham. The signalling arrangements were altered after the double junction was removed between these platforms in 1953. Now, a single-arm signal with a route-indicating apparatus below it shows drivers the state of the road ahead. In the distance is the Station signalbox and behind that the 1906 flyover. The photograph was taken in about 1964. *M. J. Lewis*

Right:
Kingham station seen from the flyover. The engine shed can be seen on the left, while the Cheltenham branch comes in on the right. The signalman has pulled off for a train on the up main line. *M. J. Lewis*

Below:
'Modified Hall' 4-6-0 No 7903 *Foremarke Hall* had just had her tank filled with water at the south end of the station when this photograph was taken on 2 September 1961. *M.Mensing*

route was, there was now a 'Direct' line from Banbury to Cheltenham (if one forgives the obligatory reversal at Chipping Norton Junction). The branch lines were worked by Train Staff and Ticket, but by 1900 the Webb-Thompson Electric Train Staff had been installed in Chipping Norton Junction North signalbox to work the section to Chipping Norton, and by 1906 the sections to Bourton were similarly controlled.

The B&CDR through trains numbered six in each direction for very many years, the timetables for 1890 and 1900 being very similar. In addition to the 12 through trains calling at the junction there were the 12 locals to Chipping Norton and the locals to Bourton. The through trains were slow.

The fastest in 1900 was the 4.17pm Banbury to Cheltenham which travelled from Banbury to Chipping Norton Junction in 45min (an average speed of 26.6mph), took only 10min to run round its train and departed relatively promptly for Cheltenham. Coming the other way, the best train, faced with the climb out of the Severn valley, averaged only 22mph, taking 63min from Cheltenham to the junction. Others took as much as 91min and then hung around at Chipping Norton Junction for 25min before continuing. Work at the station was the typical mixture of wonderful Cotswold silence and noisy activity. An example of a 'rush' period at Chipping Norton Junction in 1900 is outlined below.

Train	7.10am Banbury	6.10am Stourbridge	6.50am Cheltenham	8.25am Chipping Norton	5.30am Paddington		
Class	A	A	A	Mixed	A		
Arr	8.05am	8.08am	8.11am	8.35am	8.37am	Goods	Mixed
Dep	8.52am	8.10am	8.22am	—	8.40am	9.00am	9.00am
To	Cheltenham	Paddington	Banbury		Wolverhampton	Cheltenham	Chipping Norton

Above:
The view north from the down main platform at Kingham c1954. A '72XX' 2-8-2T is hauling a heavy freight train out of the up sidings while a BR Standard '2MT' 2-6-0 simmers outside the engine shed which was built in 1913. Note the unusual signal bracket. The arms are underslung to be seen from a distance below the station footbridge and are centrally pivoted to reduce the amount by which they encroach on headroom when lowered. The left-hand arm routes to the Cheltenham line.
P. G. Barlow/Author's Collection

Right:
A timeless scene at Kingham. 'Castle' 4-6-0 No 7007 Great Western simmers quietly with the 3.15pm Paddington to Hereford as the passengers sort themselves out on a fine July evening in 1962. Over on the branch platform the Chipping Norton connection which was brought in by 2-6-2T No 4101 is being shunted to form the connection out of the express for Cheltenham. B. J. Ashworth

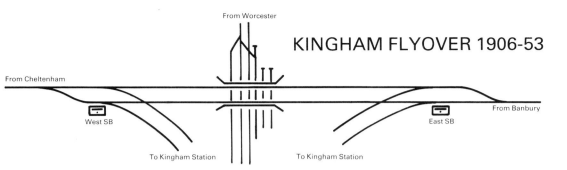

KINGHAM FLYOVER 1906-53

From Worcester

From Cheltenham

West SB

From Banbury

East SB

To Kingham Station

To Kingham Station

The GWR purchased the tracks of the B&CDR (for which it had always provided motive power and stock) in 1897 at a time when the Manchester, Sheffield & Lincolnshire Railway (MS&LR) was building its extension from Nottingham to London. At the request of the GWR, and with a loan from that company, the MS&LR constructed an 8-mile, double track railway from Culworth Junction, 2½ miles south of their Woodford & Hinton station, to the GWR's line from London to Birmingham — the junction being made less than a mile north of Banbury. The MS&LR opened its extension to Marylebone in 1899 and thus became the Great Central Railway (GCR). Trains began to run from the North to the Kent and Hampshire coasts via the Culworth to Banbury link and thence via Oxford and, given time, the GWR's investment in the old B&CDR line would start to show a return.

On 8 January 1906 the GWR opened a double track flyover across their Worcester line a little way north of Chipping Norton Junction and this, together with a new west to south curve near Lansdown Junction, opened the way for express passenger running between the GCR, Banbury, South Wales and the West of England. At once, one express train in each direction was inaugurated, each comprising six coaches of which one was a dining car. One set was provided by the GWR, the other by the GCR and their dining car was a massive 12-wheeler. The companies took the job seriously and the schedules demanded average speeds of 40-45mph between slowings to pick up the staff — no mean feat of haulage over such a dreadful road. These trains ran between Newcastle and Barry but in the 1920s were extended to Swansea.

With the inauguration of the flyover came the

Above:
The south end of the station in 1955 with the signal lowered for Collett '2251' 0-6-0 No 2202 to proceed towards Oxford from the Chipping Norton branch. Note the rear view of a GWR symmetrically balanced signal, which would route trains to the sidings ahead. It was later replaced by a tubular steel signal with an elevated ground disc.
P. G. Barlow/Author's Collection

Below:
The south end of Kingham station about 1960. The station was well supplied with water columns on the up and down main platforms and on the branch. Note the signal with the elevated disc replacing the one featured in the previous photograph. *Jim Russell*

use of slip coaches on the main line. From 1906 the crack, non-stop 1.40pm Paddington to Worcester slipped a coach at the junction for the Cheltenham line. The coach stopped at 3.14pm, thus giving an average speed of 54mph for the 84¾ uphill miles. Chipping Norton Junction staff needed to be quick off the mark as they had just 6min to attach the slipped coach to the back or the front of the 3.20pm departure. The coach returned to the junction next day on the noon departure from Cheltenham, and on arrival at the junction it was uncoupled and attached to the 11.25am Worcester to Paddington stopping train. In 1908 and until 1910 the 6.15pm Paddington to Wolverhampton also slipped a coach at the junction, but from 1910 the whole train called at the station. The 1908 service gave 10 main line passenger trains calling in the down direction and 11 on the up line. There were five stopping trains each way on the

Cheltenham branch and 10 each way towards Chipping Norton. Of these, two each way ran through to Banbury and were worked by auto or push-pull train.

In 1909 the station's name was changed to plain Kingham with no mention of the large junction which it was. In 1913 an engine shed with accommodation for two tank engines was erected in brick in the 'V' of the junction between the main line and the Chipping Norton branch. The table below gives details of the station's performance, the best figures being those between 1903 and 1923.

	Staff	Paybill £	Income £	Tickets	General merchandise Fwd (tons)	Rec (tons)	Cattle fwd
1903	23	1,213	6,275	21,925	1,416	1,749	281
1913	23	1,662	6,643	21,071	1,120	1,588	369
1923	22	3,287	10,938	22,629 (52)	1,043	1,217	495
1929	20	2,896	8,488	14,517 (48)	936	981	462
1930	20	2,857	8,658	12,396 (58)	865	1,047	470
1933	16	2,364	5,415	9,112 (43)	512	—	205
1938	16	2,506	6,621	13,106 (52)	207	—	122

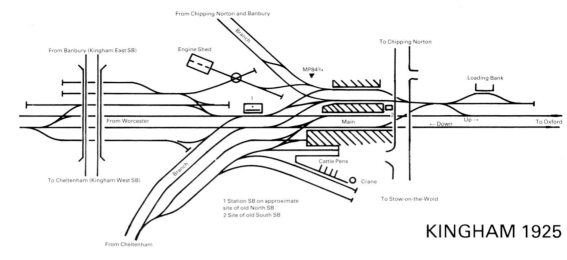

From Chipping Norton and Banbury

From Banbury (Kingham East SB)

Engine Shed

To Chipping Norton

MP84¾

Loading Bank

1

From Worcester

Main

Down →

Up →

To Oxford

Branch

To Cheltenham (Kingham West SB)

Cattle Pens

Crane

1 Station SB on approximate
site of old North SB
2 Site of old South SB

To Stow-on-the-Wold

From Cheltenham

KINGHAM 1925

Slip coach working was suspended during World War 1 but was reintroduced afterwards. The last year during which any slips were made at Kingham was 1926 when the 12.45pm and 4.45pm Paddington to Worcester expresses each slipped a coach at 2.17pm and 6.34pm respectively. Because of its tortuous single track and steep inclines, the Banbury and Cheltenham direct line saw very little through traffic. The Swansea to Newcastle service did not amount to more than one train each way, except perhaps during holiday peaks when an extra might have been run, and there do not appear to have been more than two through freight trains a day going over the flyover. The great deterrent to using the line was the need for double-heading and the difficulties and dangers of holding heavy trains back on the steep gradients.

Iron ore trains from Irthlingborough to South Wales via Yarnton came through Kingham and occasionally took the Cheltenham branch, but mostly they went on to Honeybourne and reversed there for South Wales. Iron ore trains from Banbury and Hook Norton quarries used to go over the bridge at Kingham, stop at the West box and reverse back into the station to continue their journey to Wales over easier grades. A larger number did this than went through.

When the flyover was opened Chipping Norton Junction had signalboxes named after the four points of the compass. The South box had a lever frame numbered to 33 and the North box frame was numbered to 91. The South box was abolished from 4 November 1922 and its work was taken over by the North box without a bigger frame being provided, so far as is known, so that the original frame must have had a good number of spare levers. There was no train of any type scheduled to pass over the flyover in 1947 and in September 1953 the East and West boxes were

abolished. The route over the bridge was retained merely as part of an engine-turning triangle and in due course even this was removed. However, the years 1953-56 were without doubt those with the most intense scheduled service through Kingham as the table below indicates.

Passenger trains at Kingham

Year		1908	1936	1954
Main line	up	11	7	16
	down	10	7	15
Cheltenham	arr	5	5	6
	dep	5	5	5
Chipping Norton	arr	10	5	5
	dep	10	5	5

During summer weekdays in 1954, 14 up and 16 down freight trains passed Kingham while nine down and 10 up freights were booked to stop at the junction either to work or to get out of the way of following faster trains. When translated into bell codes and lever movements, these, with the through expresses, made Kingham box an excellently busy place to work, especially with the additional job of fetching and carrying the electric token for the branch trains.

It was around 1953-54 that a diesel railcar took its first working on the Chipping Norton line, coming down from Oxford and, on its return to the junction, going on towards Honeybourne. By this time the passenger service from Kingham did not go beyond Chipping Norton; it was withdrawn on the section through to King's Sutton on 4 June 1951. The Cheltenham branch passenger service was withdrawn on 15 October 1962 and that between Kingham and Chipping Norton on 3 December 1962. A goods service ran through from Banbury to Kingham and from Kingham as far as Bourton-on-the-Water until 7 September 1964.

Like many stations, Kingham enjoyed a postwar boom and the 1950s were busier than any other time in its history. In memory of happier days it is pleasant to note that 1953 saw as many passengers at Kingham as in 1903 and 1959 saw more tickets sold than in 1923, as shown below.

Year	Income £	Tickets	General merchandise Fwd (tons)	Rec (tons)	Cattle (full wagons) fwd
1953	7,077 (132)	21,995 (80)	688	132	17
1955	7,375 (95)	23,594 (55)	102	175	12
1959	10,480 (882)	27,992 (516)	nil	334	3

Right:
The station seen from the engine shed about 1960. A magnificent tank for locomotive water stands on the left while on the right the grounded body of an old coach provides accommodation for locomotive crews. *Jim Russell*

Below:
The view east from Kingham East signalbox about 1952. Close to the camera is the electric train token setting down post or 'cow's horn' with a net to stop the token carrier swinging and a lamp to light the 'cow's horn' at night. Along the line the junction signal routes trains either 'over the bridge' or 'into the station'. The latter arm has the Kingham Station box distant fixed below it. *Jim Russell*

Most of these passengers were carried to their destinations in GWR coaches hauled by GWR steam engines; there were a few GWR diesel railcars in the workings. Some idea of how busy Kingham could be, may be obtained by looking at the following table.

Morning trains at Kingham — summer weekdays 1954												
Train	7.20 Ch N	6.25 Chelt	6.50 Oxfd	6.35 Wos				7.30 Eve	7.45 Oxfd	7.15 Gt M		7.30 Eve	8.45 Ch C
Class	B	B	B	A	B	B	B	H	B	A	G	H	C
Arr	7.30	7.35	7.37	7.45				8.34	8.34	8.39 n/s			9.00 B
Dep				7.47 To Padd	7.48 To Ch N	7.51 To Chelt	8.15 To Ch C		8.38 To Wos		8.45 To MM	8.48 To Y'ton	9.05 To Didcot

Ch N	Chipping Norton		Y'ton	Yarnton Junction
Ch C	Chipping Campden		A	Express passenger train
Wos	Worcester		B	Stopping passenger train
Eve	Evesham		C	Empty coaching stock train
Gt M	Great Malvern		G	Light engine
MM	Moreton-in-the-Marsh		H	Unbraked, through goods train

The 8.15 departure was the school train and returned from Chipping Campden as empty coaches to form the 9.05 to Didcot.

Left:
'Castle' class No 7004 *Eastnor Castle* arriving at Kingham with the 4.05pm Hereford-Worcester-Paddington on 11 May 1963.
B. J. Ashworth

Below:
In 1906 a bridge was built to carry the Banbury to Cheltenham direct line over the Oxford to Worcester main line. It lies forlornly derelict in this photograph which was taken about 1964. *M. J. Lewis*

Leominster

Leominster station was part of the properly independent Shrewsbury & Hereford Railway and lay 38½ miles south of Shrewsbury and 12½ miles north of Hereford. The railway had been laid to the standard gauge and was single track throughout when it was opened to all traffic from Shrewsbury to Ludlow, a distance of 27½ miles, on 21 April 1852 and on to Hereford, Barrs Court (the existing BR WR station) for goods traffic only on 30 July of that year. Passenger trains did not run into Barrs Court until 6 December 1853. The engines, rolling stock and men to work the line came from the Shrewsbury & Chester Railway until 1 July 1854 when Thomas Brassey, the contractor who had actually built the line, took an eight-year lease of it and worked it with his own vehicles. He managed the line so well that he paid enough rent to the S&HR for that concern to pay its shareholders a 6% dividend on their ordinary

Above:
Leominster station up side buildings seen from the road c1964. *M. J. Lewis*

shares in 1860. When Brassey's lease ran out the line was leased to the LNWR, GWR and West Midland Railways (WMR) from 1 July 1862, the line by that time having been doubled from Shrewsbury to Ludlow. The WMR was absorbed into the GWR from 1 August 1863 leaving the arch enemies — the GWR and LNWR — as joint lessees of the route in the form of the 'London & North Western and Great Western Joint Committee'. The Joint concern then set about doubling the rest of the S&HR through Leominster to Hereford. This was soon complete with the exception of the 1,067yd Dinmore tunnel which remained as single track until 1893.

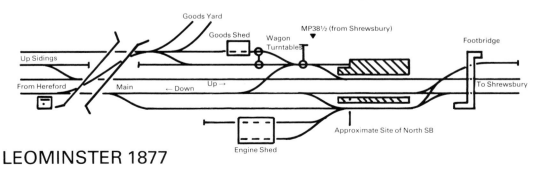

LEOMINSTER 1877

Leominster became a junction station on 20 August 1857 when the line to Kington was opened from a junction 34 chains north of Leominster. The branch was single tracked, 13¼ miles long, and was leased and worked by Thomas Brassey until the WMR took over on 1 July 1862. The other branch line from Leominster was one of the sleepiest that the GWR ever had the misfortune to operate, namely that which ran across country through Bromyard to Leominster

Junction which lay 4 miles from Worcester on the line to Hereford.

The idea of linking Leominster to Worcester did not appeal to investors and the route was 23 years in the making. The first section from Leominster Junction to Yearsett was seven miles long and terminated four miles short of Bromyard. This was opened on 1 May 1874 and Yearsett remained the terminus until 22 October 1877 when the line was opened to Bromyard. On 1 March 1884 a branch from Leominster was opened. It ran parallel to the down main line for 1¼ miles, going towards Hereford, crossed a river and then turned sharply east into the Herefordshire hills. The effort of climbing past the village of Stoke Prior proved too much and the line stopped at Steen's Bridge where the Leominster to Bromyard road crossed the rails. A passenger joining the train at Leominster was taken for a four-mile ride and put out of his carriage 3¼ miles (by road) from his starting place. When the railway was completed between Steen's Bridge and Bromyard and opened on 1 September 1897, the rail distance from the bridge to Bromyard was nine miles and the road distance eight miles.

With the opening of the line, Leominster became a five-platform station. The up main line trains, ie those travelling towards Shrewsbury, used Platform 1 which was nearest the town. Down main line trains used Platform 2 and trains from Kington went around the back of Platform 2 to Platform 3. The Bromyard line trains had Platforms 4 and 5, each side of an 'island', all to themselves, but this was sheer optimism on behalf of the line's owners and Platform 5 became a siding.

Including that at Kington Junction there were then three signalboxes at Leominster. Kington Junction, 34 chains north of the station, was a small, brick box in that distinctive if somewhat crude style of the LNWR/GWR Joint Committee. It contained 20 levers and a gate wheel for working the gates across the main road. Levers 17, 18 and 19 each worked an up distant signal but in more recent times distant signal 19 was fitted with an electric motor switched on automatically after distant 18 had been lowered and thus lever 19 became a spare.

The original Leominster station signalbox had 35 levers and stood on the down platform. It was replaced by a larger box in 1901 when the layout of the station was enlarged. The replacement was a big timber box, built to an LNWR design, which stood above the down platform supported by a massive steel gantry. In 1919 the LNWR lever frame was replaced by a GWR frame of levers numbered to 91. Positioned 567yd to the south was Leominster South End signalbox — another squat, LNWR/GWR Joint structure housing a 20-lever frame in a floor 15ft square. The levers must have been widely spaced because in July 1941, due to the enlargement of the goods yard, the GWR installed a 35-lever frame without increasing the size of the box. The Bromyard branch passed close behind the South End box but was not in any way controlled from that box, the block section being from Leominster station to Fencote. The second engine shed at Leominster was opened in 1901. It was a standard Swindon product in brick with a northlight roof over two roads and a floor space of 50ft×40ft. The Leominster branches seem to have been worked largely by 0-4-2Ts and the occasional saddle tank. For many years Nos 5807 and 5817 were Leominster engines, before, during and after the war right up to 1957.

The Kington branch always seemed to be the

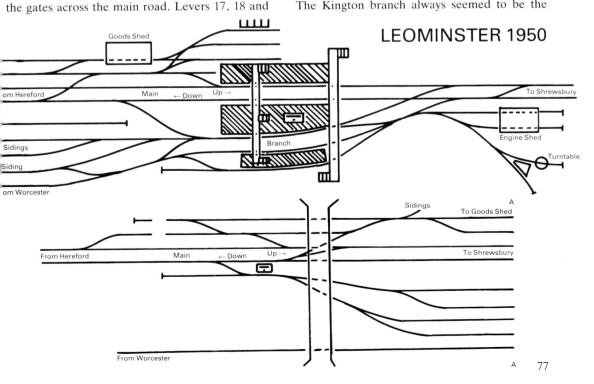

LEOMINSTER 1950

livelier of the two. In 1908 there were nine passenger and freight trips each way to Kington with three Station Trucks — Nos ST7, ST671 and ST672. ST7 worked between Paddington and Kington via Shrewsbury and arrived each morning at Leominster on the 5.05am Oxley to Hereford goods. ST672 worked between Presteigne and Shrewsbury, being shunted off or on to a main line goods at Leominster South End, while ST671 had a circular tour, apparently, which involved it working up the Midland line from Eardisley Junction to Hereford and then back to Eardisley via Leominster, where it was shunted off into South End, and on to a branch train for Titley Junction and Eardisley. This truck would carry whatever required a prompt delivery, rather like the 'Red Star' parcels service of today.

Freight arrived at Leominster South End throughout the small hours and up to breakfast time and the shunters with a pilot engine supplied from Leominster shed would be kept busy breaking up rakes of wagons off trains from the branches and the main lines. This was the case in 1900, when the pilot engine was booked out six days a week and it was still the case in 1950. One of the best vantage points for watching trains at Leominster, say those who had the luck to be able to use them, was on the Bromyard road bridge, overlooking the entire yard to the north and within earshot of the signal bells on the south side of the bridge.

There were, in 1908 (and the system changed little over the years) five down main line and six up main line goods trains which called at Leominster yard. Twelve express trains ran through (six each way) and there were 13 stopping trains in each direction — some GWR, some LNWR and some

run for the Joint Company. As a general rule no 'A' class train, other than a down mail, stopped at any intermediate station on the Shrewsbury and Hereford route, until during or after World War 2. Passengers for Leominster changed into the stopping train at Shrewsbury or Hereford, the latter leaving a few minutes after the fast.

In 1900-08 the through trains appear to have had a limited number of destinations; they all came down either from Liverpool or Manchester and went to Cardiff, Paignton, Plymouth or Penzance. Over the years the West Country destinations became more varied. These were heavy, important trains running over a difficult secondary main line and they came through Leominster behind some of the biggest engines of the day — be that a big 2-4-0 in 1900, a Churchward 'County' Class 4-4-0 in 1908 or a 'Saint' 4-6-0 in 1930. Up trains came through Leominster 'hard against the collar' on a nagging 1 in 400 gradient up the long and ever steepening climb to Church Stretton summit. On summer Saturdays in the 1920s, 1930s or 1950s, there were around 28 expresses scheduled through plus any excursions or other seasonal extras and then there was such a procession of powerful express engines as would delight the heart of any enthusiast. 'Royal Scots', 'Stars', 'Black Fives', 'Castles', 'Patriots' and 'Granges' all came through while in the South End yard maybe a 'Super D' 0-8-0 was waiting for No 5817 to finish shunting wagons and allow the big engine to continue its journey.

The weekday express service in 1936 was 14 fast trains, seven each way, with eight stopping trains — a reduction on 1908 typical of the 1930s. The Bromyard branch had five passenger trains each way with one freight from Worcester and back and an extra train from Leominster to Bromyard and

Left:
A sooty and well-worn signalbox testifies to 50 years of hard working locomotives. The Bromyard branch train prepares for its journey to Worcester on the sunny afternoon of 24 July 1951. *R. C. Riley*

Right:
Leominster Station box with some window frames removed and its gantry spanning empty track beds c1964. *M. J. Lewis*

Below right:
Many types of locomotive, from LNWR 'Super D' 0-8-0s to little GWR 0-4-2Ts took water at Leominster. This photograph, taken about 1964, shows the main water storage tank which fed the station columns resting on the massive walls of the pumping house. Handsome, solid, British engineering which the British were later to demolish. *M. J. Lewis*

Below:
Coming down the gradient with a Shrewsbury-Bristol express on 24 July 1951, 'Castle' 4-6-0 No 7000 *Viscount Portal* is about to raise the dust through Leominster station. The station nameboard used to bear the legend LEOMINSTER change here for KINGTON, NEW RADNOR, PRESTEIGNE and BROMYARD lines. *R. C. Riley*

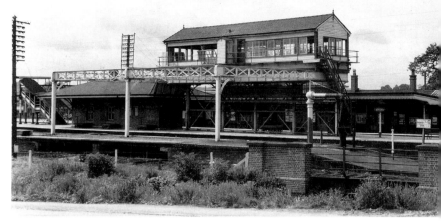

back once a fortnight on Fair days. There were no Station Trucks. The 6.18am to Kington was an interesting working. It ran down as a mixed train, and, coupled ahead of the freight brake van was a passenger Brake Third carrying the Kington mails which 30min earlier had been put out of a down main line mail and passenger train. The three Station Trucks were still running and they went down together on the 8.20am goods.

The branch trains were worked by Kington, Leominster and Worcester engines hauling coaches — auto-trains did not feature in the workings until during or after World War 2. The 8.05am Worcester passenger train arrived at Leominster via Bromyard behind a Worcester 2-4-0T or more usually an 0-4-2T at 9.26am. The men uncoupled from the train at the No 3 platform and took their engine to shed where they turned it, took water and refilled their bunker. This involved filling a ½-ton bucket at the coaling stage and hoisting the fuel aloft with the hand-winched crane prior to dropping it dustily into the engine's bunker. They then cleared up the mess on the footplate and on the ground around before going back to their train and continuing bunker first, with a load of fresh coal piled high on a practically cabless locomotive, as the 9.56 Leominster to New Radnor. They were right to be chimney first for the

longer haul back from New Radnor to Worcester. By 1947 two of the five round trips on the Bromyard line were worked by diesel railcars, while down from Wooferton Junction came other diesels, extending their earlier working between Kidderminster, Bewdley, Tenbury and Wooferton. Also in 1947, or a little before, at least one auto-coach was allocated to Leominster and an 0-4-2T worked this over ground hitherto unseen by Leominster engines. Starting off at 7.22am the Leominster auto-train went up to Wooferton and along the Wyre Forest line as far as Tenbury before returning to Leominster at 9.08am to work the 9.50am to New Radnor and then coming back to Leominster again for a trip to Tenbury.

The Leominster to Bromyard section was closed on 15 September 1952. The Kington branch closed to passenger traffic on 7 February 1955 and to goods in September 1957. Leominster station box was abolished on 31 May 1964 but the South End box — ancient, ugly and well over 100 years old — is still in use in 1987. Leominster station remains in use — a scruffy shadow of its former self, weed grown and awful, stripped of just about everything that makes a railway station interesting. In an attempt to leave some impression of what the place was like in its heyday, a compilation from the 1951 working timetable is laid out below.

Leominster Connections 1951 — weekdays 7.00am-9.00am
(12 trains per hour or one every 5min)

		2.30am	3.25am	7.21am	7.32am		6.25am	6.45am	5.45am		5.00am
		Cardiff	Auto	Saltney	K'ton	H'ford		Salop	Salop	P'pool		S Fk
	B	H	B	H	B	B	K	B	H	H	B	H
Arr					7.55am	7.56am		8.05am				8.59am
n/s		7.02am		7.33am					8.29am	C8.38R		
Dep 7.00am				7.22am		7.58am	8.00am	8.06am			8.45am	9.20am
To				To	To		To	To	To	To	To	
Wos				T'b'y	P'pool		Salop	K'ton	H'f'd	H'f'd	H'l'cott	Wos	P'pool

Wos	Worcester	P'pool	Pontypool Road		B	Stopping passenger train
T'b'y	Tenbury	H'f'd	Hereford		H	Unbraked through goods
K'ton	Kington	H'l'cott	Harlescott Sidings		K	Local pick-up goods

Left:
Looking north from the north end of the down platform. The William Dean-designed engine shed looks semi-derelict but is still in use. The three-doll signal's tallest arm routes trains down the main line, the middle arm is for Platform 3 and the right-hand arm for Platform 4.   *H. C. Casserley*

Below:
Collett '14XX' 0-4-2T No 1455 had arrived at Leominster with its train from Kington at 2.23pm on 24 July 1951, and is seen making a connection with the 1.15pm Shrewsbury to Hereford stopping train which is seen pulling in at 2.27pm. The latter consists of four smart GWR coaches behind an equally smart GWR 'Castle' 4-6-0 No 5073 *Blenheim* on 24 July 1951.   *R. C. Riley*

Bottom:
Looking south off the footbridge at Leominster on 24 July 1951 after the main line stopping train seen in the previous picture had gone. No 1455 blows off steam while her driver chats and waits for the engine to be uncoupled from the train. The signal is 'off' for the engine to run into the down sidings before reversing into the engine shed.   *R. C. Riley*

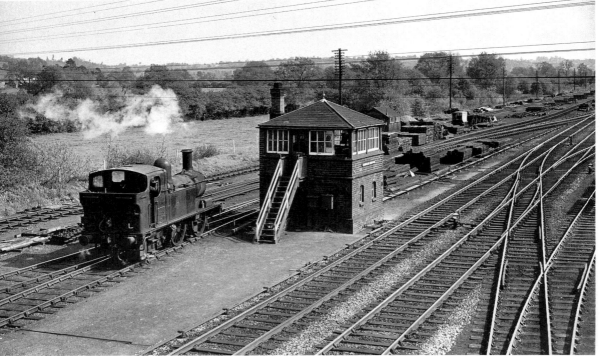

Top:
Back on Leominster shed, No 1455 now has an overflowing bunker and the men have gone off for tea and a wash. No 5807, another long-serving member of the shed, is parked tight against a coal tub to make the job of coaling her as easy as possible. In 1946-47 the hand-winched crane was working. Perhaps by 24 July 1951 it had fallen into disrepair? *R. C. Riley*

Above:
Looking south off the Bromyard road bridge. Leominster South End box, a relic from the 1870s, still stands four square by the lineside on 15 May 1964 as '14XX' 0-4-2T No 1438 shunts away down the sidings. The rails on the far left behind the engine were once part of the route to Bromyard. *B. J. Ashworth*

Right:
'Ugly and ancient' Leominster South End signalbox. This view shows well how massively strong these buildings were. After a 100 years or more the nameplate is still fixed to the wall. Handsome is as handsome does! *M. J. Lewis*

Left:
Looking north off the Bromyard road bridge over the yards at the south of the station. The tumbled sleepers of the Bromyard branch are on the right and the sadly empty sidings, once full of noise and trucks, flank the main lines. *M. J. Lewis*

Below:
What have they done to my song? Leominster station looking north over weeds and colour-light signals in 1982. The magnificent pole route remains to remind us of the old railway. *Michael H. C. Baker*

Wellington (Salop)

Above:
The exterior of Wellington station from the downside about 1954. *Lens of Sutton*

Wellington (Salop) station began life as a junction on 1 June 1849 as the joint property of the Shrewsbury & Birmingham (S&BR) and Shropshire Union Railways (SUR). The SUR came from the LNWR main line at Stafford to Shrewsbury, and formed a junction with the S&BR a little way east of Wellington station. The SUR had been leased from the outset to the LNWR so the S&BR management were brought into sharp contact with the appalling Capt Mark Huish, Chairman of the larger company. The story of the sharp practice and broken promises of the LNWR in regard to the S&BR is best read in Volume 1 of McDermott's *History of the Great Western Railway* (Ian Allan Ltd). At Wellington, Stafford Junction in July 1851, the S&BR had to remove two rails and place a strong guard of navvies over the break owing to a rumour that the LNWR was going to run a train to Wolverhampton over S&BR metals. Huish looked upon railway business as warfare, but in attempting to crush his rivals he sometimes defeated himself and in the case of the S&BR he forced it into the arms of the GWR which was then looking for a route from Birmingham to the Mersey. Wellington station became joint GWR/LNWR property, the LNWR having formally absorbed the old SUR on 1 September 1854.

The station lay 19 miles 46 chains northeast of Wolverhampton and 10¼ miles east of Shrewsbury. The Stafford junction was 27 chains (594yd)

east of the station. On 1 July 1861 a branch line from Ketley Junction, 1 mile 6 chains east of Stafford Junction, was opened to Lightmoor as part of a single track railway which would eventually go through Much Wenlock to the GWR/LNWR Joint line at Marsh Farm Junction, just north of Craven Arms, on 16 December 1867. The trains on this line as well as those to Stafford used the bay platforms at Wellington. The last junction to be made was 29 chains towards Shrewsbury. This was the start of a 16 mile 52 chain double track line to Market Drayton, where an end-on junction was made with the existing GWR branch going on to Nantwich on the LNWR Crewe-Shrewsbury line. The Nantwich-Market Drayton line had been opened on 20 October 1863 as a kind of GWR appendix attached to the LNWR, but with the opening of the Wellington-Market Drayton line on 16 October 1867, and with Parliamentary running powers over the LNWR beyond Nantwich, the GWR had a route through Crewe to Manchester London Road.

The financial and maintenance arrangements at a Joint station were always wondrously complicated as each company made sure that the other paid its full share, right down to the cost of gas light in the refreshment rooms and signalboxes.

84

An official survey of 1892 shows that the turntable at Wellington was Joint property with the siding leading to it but the engine shed and its approach tracks were GWR-owned while all around the sidings were Joint property — except for the one set of points which switched locomotives on to the fan of engine shed sidings. The engine shed is believed to have been a converted goods shed — the alterations were carried out in 1876 and the building was in use until 10 August 1964. The 19th century coaling deck with its crane for lifting and swinging buckets of coal fell into disuse in the 1950s and was replaced by a very temporary-looking structure with an electrically operated coal hoist.

The station's layout was controlled by four signalboxes numbered from 1 to 4 from the east or London end. Thus Stafford Junction was controlled by No 1 box, Nos 2 and 3 boxes were at each end of the platforms — No 2 on the up side and No 3 on the down — and No 4 box worked Market Drayton Junction. All four were constructed to a 'Mk 2' signalbox plan at the GWR/LNWR Joint Company's office in Birkenhead. An example of the 'Mk 1' design can be seen in the previous section on Leominster. The Wellington boxes were handsome but yet retaining that 'massiveness' associated with the LNWR. They seem to have been a happy cross-breed of LNWR and Saxby & Farmer practice with just a

Above:
Looking towards Shrewsbury on the down platform about 1954. The corner of No 3 signalbox can be seen just off the platform end.
Lens of Sutton

WELLINGTON c1900

Above:
The 7.05pm Much Wenlock to Wellington standing by No 3 box behind 2-6-2T No 4178. This was the last train on the last day of the passenger service from Much Wenlock on 21 July 1962. No 3 signalbox was built to the 1880s standard pattern Joint line design — heavily influenced as this was by Saxby & Farmer. *M. Mensing*

Left:
The signalman in No 3 box has stopped a down freight on the middle road to allow Ivatt '2MT', 2-6-2T to leave the down bay with the 2.35pm to Crewe via Market Drayton on 9 June 1962. The freight is hauled by '28XX' 2-8-0 No 2866. On the cylinder cover there are some interesting chalkings made by a fitter, one of which states that the 'latest bore size' is 19.996in. The nominal diameter of a '28XX' cylinder is 18.5in so this would have been a very powerful engine, albeit somewhat greedy for coal.
M. Mensing

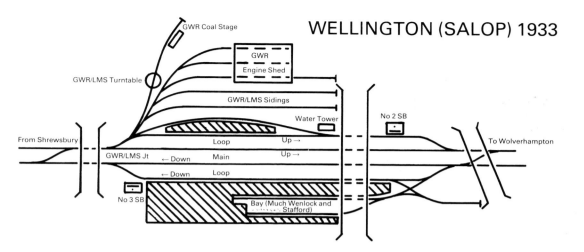

WELLINGTON (SALOP) 1933

GWR Coal Stage

GWR Engine Shed

GWR/LMS Turntable

GWR/LMS Sidings

Water Tower

No 2 SB

From Shrewsbury

To Wolverhampton

GWR/LMS Jt

Loop

Up →

Up →

← Down   Main

← Down   Loop

No 3 SB

Bay (Much Wenlock and Stafford)

touch of GWR for good measure. The No 1 box was in place by 1886 and had 22 levers to control a simple double junction. The levers were placed at 5½in centres and were interlocked by a Saxby & Farmer rocker and grid machine. This box was closed on 10 September 1967. No 2 box was in place by 1886 and was replaced by a London Midland Region brick walled, flat roofed box on 15 March 1953. This box had a lever frame numbered to 71. No 3 box was in use by 1886. Its floor space, which measured 33ft 5in×10ft 3in, was raised 6ft 9in above the rails and contained a frame of levers numbered to 58 with LNWR tappet interlocking. Wellington No 4 signalbox measured 27ft 3in×15ft 3in inside. It was in use by 1886 and in September 1955 the old frame was replaced with a Western Region standard locking frame with levers numbered to 46. Nos 3 and 4 boxes were closed on 30 September 1973.

The goods yard at Wellington flanked the up and down main lines between Nos 3 and 4 boxes, with the LNWR/LMS accommodation on the up side and the GWR on the down. There were no facing points from either main line into the yards and throughout the station's history freight trains had to reverse into the yards and in so doing would have had to cross a main line. An up GWR goods

with work to do at Wellington would have stopped in the station and backed across the down main to the yard at No 3 box. A down LNWR/LMS goods would have stopped with the tail of the train clear of the crossing at No 4 box and then reversed over into the yard. The signalman could not just reverse a train into either yard without consulting the yard staff to see if (a) the way was clear and (b) if they could deal with the train at that time. Both the 1903 and the 1933 printed instructions state that the signalman was to summon the yard foreman for consultations by blowing for him on a specially provided horn — and in the meantime the up or down main line was occupied by a stationary goods train, blocking it for through passenger movements. The instructions permitted the station's platform loops and through tracks to be used when a goods train had to be reversed out of the goods yard. Maybe the train had to continue a northbound journey but the northern exit from the yard was blocked. The only time such a movement could not be made was when a passenger train was moving in the station. Trips of goods wagons could be made through the station without a brake van at the rear. With the busy service scheduled for the station it would appear to have been a difficult and interesting one to work at or to sit and watch.

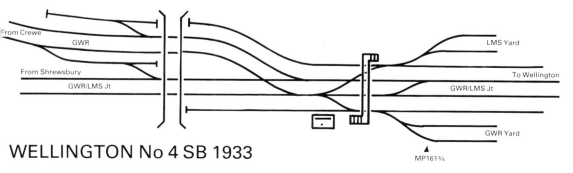

From Crewe

GWR

LMS Yard

From Shrewsbury

To Wellington

GWR/LMS Jt

GWR/LMS Jt

GWR Yard

WELLINGTON No 4 SB 1933

MP161¾

Before World War 1, three down expresses from Paddington slipped a coach at Wellington for Manchester. The coach was slipped at No 1 box and, while the main train went through the Middle Road at Wellington, the slip guard brought his coach to a stand at the No 2 box down home signal. When it had stopped, the facing points were set for the platform loop and an engine came out from the platform to draw the coach in. The trains concerned were the 11.25am, 2.15pm and 4.55pm expresses from Paddington. The first two were scheduled to average 43mph between London and Wellington, taking all stops into account, and the 4.55pm was booked to run at an overall average speed of 41mph. The trains offered to Wellington passengers in 1903-14 provided a comprehensive service but speeds were low. The fastest train between Wolverhampton and Wellington, the 11.25am in 1908, averaged 39mph non-stop while the rest, calling at some or all stations, averaged 20-27mph.

Throughout the years 1900-55, the service was mainly from Paddington to Shrewsbury and Birkenhead with the branches feeding in and out of the main trunk route. As the years passed the number of main line 'A' class trains increased while the local main line and the branch services decreased — the difference between 1908 and 1955 in this respect is most marked. Before World War 1 the Market Drayton branch was almost a secondary main line as slip coaches and the rear

halves of other Paddington expresses were worked over that route through to Manchester. Some trains actually went to Manchester by both routes, the front half going via Shrewsbury and Birkenhead and the rear, detached at Wellington, going on through Market Drayton. The 8.30am Birmingham and the 6.30am Paddington expresses are examples. In the opposite direction there were four trains from Manchester to Market Drayton and Wellington which were attached to Birkenhead to Paddington expresses and one, the 9.15am Crewe, which worked through to Paddington — doubtless with a change of engine somewhere along the line. However, the majority of trains on the Market Drayton line were freights, there being 56 per day against 22 passenger trains. Passengers flocked to the station as shown below.

	Staff	Paybill £	Income £	Tickets
1903	—	—	14,801	213,008
1913	39	—	15,743	197,953

According to these figures, in 1903 the booking office was selling tickets at an average rate of one every 2½min, day and night, throughout the year. On the freight side during the same period the performance was equally good, as the following statistics will confirm.

	Staff	Paybill £	Income £	General merchandise		Cattle fwd
				Fwd (tons)	Rec (tons)	
1903	—	—	13,310	7,330	7,811	3,187
1913	26	1,813	16,228	10,306	10,336	3,538

The total income in 1913 was nearly nine times greater than the money paid in wages to the GWR goods station staff. After World War 1 the performance of the passenger and the freight stations slumped as shown below.

	Staff	Paybill £	Income £	General merchandise		Cattle fwd
				Fwd (tons)	Rec (tons)	
1923	30	4,717	19,857	5,591	9,473	1,805
1929	31	4,611	17,613	4,579	8,769	2,445
1930	27	4,843	16,446	3,420	8,708	2,319
1933	Staff now paid		14,572	2,435	9,153	1,622
1938	by LM&S Co		12,731	1,505	7,802	1,396

Income in 1923 was 4.21 times greater than the paybill but this had dropped by 1930 to 3.39 times. Revenue was falling and costs were rising. The situation was the same at the passenger station.

	Staff	Paybill £	Income £	Tickets	Ratio of income to paybill
1923	45	7,851	27,195	180,008 (462)	3.46 : 1
1929	40	7,121	26,152	157,586 (551)	3.67 : 1
1930	39	7,214	24,945	154,815 (508)	3.45 : 1
1933	36	6,367	20,496	128,132 (433)	3.21 : 1
1938	36	7,033	25,145	169,639 (607)	3.57 : 1

(Figures in brackets are the number of season tickets sold.)

Left:
Locomotive accommodation, preparation, and disposal facilities were not the best at Wellington. The place seems to have been neglected even to the extent of a goods shed being converted into an engine shed in 1876, and this sufficed until the end. This was the windswept coaling area on 13 December 1958, with '57XX' 0-6-0PT No 3732 in attendance. *M. Mensing*

In an area of growing population the passenger figures were maintained after a fall but freight was gradually draining away as a rural area became more urbanised.

In 1955 Wellington station was enjoying the busiest service ever although it was slightly less complicated in that the slip coaches had been abandoned 30 years or more previously and there were no through trains between Paddington and Crewe or through coaches to Manchester via Market Drayton. There were more 'A' class trains between Shrewsbury or Birkenhead and Paddington than ever before and, with all the branches still running, Wellington was still a thriving junction. Sad to say, the Much Wenlock branch trains were sometimes timed to just miss their rightful connection to Crewe. The breakfast time connections at Wellington were as follows:

Wellington trains 7.30-8.30am — weekdays 1955

6.05am		6.50am Much	7.30am	6.30am	7.45am	7.20am	
Crewe		Wenlock	Salop	Birmingham	Salop	Stafford	
B	B	B	A	B	B	B	B
Arr 7.28am		7.35am	7.44am	8.00am	8.05am	8.03am	
Dep	7.30am		7.45am		8.06am	8.06am	8.30am
	To		To		To	To	To
	Crewe		Paddington		Stafford	Salop	Wolverhampton

The overall average speed of the expresses and the local trains was practically unchanged from 1908-40 — 46mph for the 'A' class trains and 20-30mph for the 'B' class. There were far more cross-country services in 1955 than at any time before, including Birkenhead to Dover or Bournemouth trains and an unexpected service from Worcester to Crewe via Market Drayton. In 24hr in 1955, 94 passenger, milk or parcels trains and 94 goods trains called at or ran through Wellington, 28 of the latter working in the yards. To deal with the carriage and freight shunting, six pilot engines were scheduled to be on duty, though not all at the same time, to provide shunting power at the station from 7am until 11pm. The table below gives an idea of what the interested observer might have seen during his lunch break on Wellington's platforms.

	A	F	G	K	B	F	B	B	K	B	A
Arr				1.17			1.35	1.43	1.46	1.48	1.58
n/s	1.04	1.10				1.35					
Dep			1.15		1.30			1.46			2.02
	1	2	3	4	5	6	7	8	9	10	11

1 10.10am Paddington-Birkenhead
2 9.07am Worcester-Market Drayton
3 Light engine to Shrewsbury
4 12.45pm Hadley
5 To Wolverhampton
6 Noon Crewe-Stourbridge Junction
7 12.50pm Wolverhampton
8 1.04pm Stafford-Salop
9 11.50am Shrewsbury
10 1.00pm Much Wenlock
11 11.45am Birkenhead-Paddington

Left:
Immediately beyond the bridge by No 3 box, the tracks fanned out into extensive sidings with freight facilities for the GWR on the down side and the LNWR on the up side. The 10.00am Wellington to Crewe via Market Drayton is passing the GWR cattle pens on 30 March 1959 as 'Castle' 4-6-0 No 5001 *Llandovery Castle* approaches tender first with empty coaches. Above the engine is the LNWR goods shed which on that date was still carrying its LNWR name of Wellington, Queen Street. *M. Mensing*

Above:
Further on down the line trains came to Wellington No 4 box or Market Drayton Junction. Here, '56XX' 0-6-2T No 5690 is heading away down the line towards Shrewsbury with a shunting trip on 4 July 1959. The line to Market Drayton diverges to the right. *M. Mensing*

Left:
The view looking back to No 4 box and the station as Stanier 'Black Five' 4-6-0 No 45004 approaches with the 3.54pm Stafford to Shrewsbury stopping train on 4 July 1959. The Crewe line can just be seen on the left. *M. Mensing*

Above:
The outlook obtained when facing the opposite way from the same position as in the previous photograph. No 3732, a '57XX' 0-6-0PT, comes in with the 3.15pm Crewe to Wellington on 4 July 1959. Note the ATC ramp just ahead of the home signal on the Shrewsbury line. *M. Mensing*

Left:
At the No 2 box or east end of Wellington station, looking towards Wolverhampton from the up platform, as '28XX' 2-8-0 No 2871 passes through with an up freight on 4 July 1959. *M. Mensing*

Above right:
Looking east from the up bay platforms as '57XX' 0-6-0PT No 9630 waits to leave with the 4.30pm to Much Wenlock on 4 July 1959. The 1953-built signalbox can just be seen behind the engine's cab. *M. Mensing*

Right:
The bay platforms and their starting signals at Wellington. Note the GWR symmetrically balanced arms and elevated ground discs. The train, the 3.10pm to Much Wenlock, is headed by '57XX' 0-6-0PT No 9774 on a cold, wet 13 December 1958. *M. Mensing*

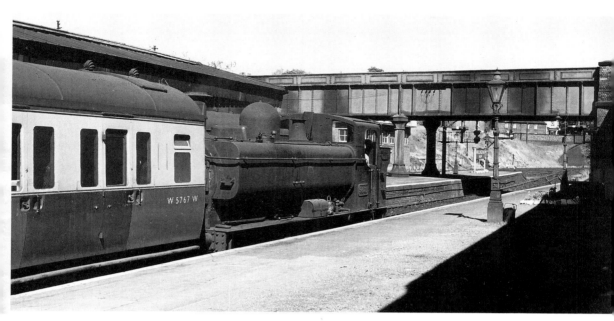

Whitland

Whitland station eventually became the junction for the entire West Wales peninsula, but it began life on 2 January 1854 as a wayside station on the broad gauge, single track South Wales Railway (SWR) serving a small market town. The railway was built as a trunk route to Milford Haven in order to carry away the boatloads of food sent out of Ireland by Irish peasants so that they might pay their rents — the basis of a succession of terrible famines. In this great design Whitland was unimportant. The single track was doubled from 1 July 1857.

On 30 July 1863 the standard gauge Pembroke & Tenby Railway (P&TR) was opened and was very successful — so much so that its management wanted to link into the rest of the nation's railway network. In pursuit of this, a 16¼-mile extension was built from Tenby to Whitland and a station built close to that of the GWR — as the SWR had now become. The P&TR hoped that the GWR would allow a third rail to be laid in the broad gauge tracks to admit the P&T trains through to Carmarthen Town where their trains could connect with the Aberystwyth trains of the Manchester & Milford Railway and the Shrewsbury trains of the LNWR. Needless to say, the GWR refused so the P&TR went to Parliament and obtained an Act which enabled them either to build their own line to Carmarthen or demand

running powers over the GWR. The GWR took the lesser of the two evils and agreed to let the P&TR through to Carmarthen on GWR metals — but at a cost of £20,000. As this was 10 times less than the cost of a new railway, the P&TR agreed. What the wicked old Great Western then did was to narrow the gauge of their up main line for the P&TR whilst retaining their down line as a broad gauge single track. As the cost of this operation was nowhere near £20,000 the GWR did well out of the deal. The P&TR then built the curve from the ex-GWR up main line into Carmarthen Town station, LNWR coaches began to run through to Pembroke, and Whitland became a junction without any real connection between the two routes from 1 July 1868.

The broad gauge was abolished on the old SWR main line during May 1872 and the peculiar arrangement of tracks between Carmarthen and

Whitland was abolished. P&TR trains no longer ran through to Carmarthen but were attached to the rear of GWR trains at Whitland. During the conversion period an arrival bay for P&TR trains was also added to the upside at Whitland and a down line departure bay was provided behind the down platform. Soon after May 1872 the P&TR's

separate station was shut. The provision of these bays was not solely for the benefit of the P&TR. The Whitland & Taff Vale Railway was then under construction. The first section from Taff Vale Junction, 2¼ miles west of Whitland, to Llanfyrnach (10½ miles) was opened on 24 March 1874. Another 3½ miles to Crymmych Arms was opened

Above:
Whitland station looking west along the up platform with the former goods shed on the left. The junction signal for the Pembroke line and down main can be seen at the far end of the platform. About 1925. *Author's Collection*

Below:
The old station building on the up platform at Whitland shortly before demolition in 1957. *Author's Collection*

in October and on 1 September 1886 the line was opened through to Cardigan, whereupon it changed its name to the Whitland & Cardigan Railway. The little 'Cardi-bach' became part of the GWR in 1890 although it had looked like a GWR branch since 1886.

The P&TR became part of the GWR in 1896. By that time the GWR was waking up and doing its best to develop traffic. Milford and Neyland in particular were developing and this improved the number of trains passing or calling at Whitland. From 1906 the new harbour at Fishguard brought the first real express trains, such as the Ocean Mails and the famous 'Day Tripper' to Killarney

from Paddington, through Whitland, hauled by the finest motive power available.

From being a remote, moorland sort of place, Whitland station developed the air of a main line junction with a busy engine shed, express passenger and freight trains thundering through, plenty of local traffic and a lot of shunting. The station was controlled by two signalboxes — East and West. Both were in use in 1868 and both survived until 2 September 1972 although the West box was rebuilt in 1902 and the East box also underwent extension and rebuilding at some stage. The East box controlled the main road level crossing and had a 21-lever frame. The West box had a 43-lever frame. From 2 September 1972 these signalboxes were abolished and a second-hand box from Danycraig with a 39-lever frame took over the functions of both with a somewhat reduced track layout.

The train service in 1908 consisted of 57 main line passenger and freight trains with six each way on the 'Cardi-bach' — including two mixed and two goods trains — and nine each way on the P&TR including two freights and a steam railmotor. The steam railmotor had been sent to Fishguard in 1907 and from there worked to Neyland and to Pembroke Dock. The railmotor

from Neyland arrived at Whitland at 10.23am allowing passengers to catch the 10.40am to Pembroke or the 10.48am to Cardigan, these two branch trains also being available to passengers off the semi-fast from Gloucester arriving at 10.25am. Express trains to and from Paddington which called at Whitland were few in 1908. The 9.15pm Paddington, known as 'Paddy's Mail', arrived at Whitland at 5.30am where the 5.50am to Cardigan and the 5.55am to Pembroke were waiting. On the up line there was the 8.05am Neyland at 9.13am taking with it passengers from the Cardigan line, together with passengers and even perhaps

Above:
Whitland West box up branch starting signals with the junction signal lowered for the bay line. East box's fixed distant is below the main line stop signal. On the left is a GWR tubular steel signal applying to the same routes as the wooden signal but to trains on the up main line. A nice contrast in styles. *Pat Garland*

Right:
Looking towards Carmarthen from the footbridge at the east end of the station in 1961. The United Dairies milk processing plant which provided so much work for the station is in the left middle distance. *John Morris*

coaches from the P&T. It was scheduled to stand at Whitland for 10min so maybe this was to give time for such coaches to be attached.

The Pembroke line had a better system of connections than the 'Cardi-bach'. The 10.50am Neyland to Paddington express and the 1pm Neyland 'North Mail' took away P&T line traffic but made no connection with the Cardigan line. However, the last up train from Cardigan arrived at Whitland at 7.10pm and connected with the very important 6.30pm Neyland to Paddington Mail as did the last up P&T line train. It is interesting to notice how trains ran on the branches, for, apart from having to meet overnight trains from England, they tended to run at godly hours. People lived closer to their work and travel was a 'journey' rather than 'commuting'. Six trains were real daily 'events' at Whitland before World War 1. These were the expresses that galloped through non-stop — among them the very famous, very fast 8.45am and 8.45pm Paddington to Fishguard Irish boat trains and, perhaps even more special, the 9.25am Pembroke Dock to Paddington express which came storming off the branch to run non-stop through the station. Six goods trains stopped to cut off and take up traffic at Whitland, quite apart from the coming and going of the local branch goods. The entire area was becoming more prosperous before World War 1 — the following table gives Whitland's traffic figures; the increase in travel will be noted and thereby the inference of greater local prosperity.

	Staff	Paybill £	Income £	Tickets	General merchandise Fwd (tons)	Rec (tons)	Cattle fwd
1903	40	2,046	8,668	33,226	1,241	3,638	593
1913	36	2,731	10,805	40,255	1,261	4,416	745

Top right:
Rather a long way from its 'natural' home, 'Manor' 4-6-0 No 7825 *Lechlade Manor* runs into Whitland with the 1.10pm Pembroke to Paddington, the 'Pembroke Coast Express', right time at 2.27pm on a summer's day in 1961.
John Stimpson/Author's Collection

Below:
Arriving light from Carmarthen in 1961, 'Castle' 4-6-0 No 5098 *Clifford Castle* will be turned on Whitland's turntable and come back through the station to work one of the famous 'Whitland Milk' trains up to Wood Lane near Kensington. *John Stimpson/Author's Collection*

Right:
The 'Pembroke Coast Express' was booked to stop for 5min at Whitland, thus allowing plenty of time for the photographer to get on to the east end footbridge for his shot of the train leaving.
John Stimpson/Author's Collection

After World War 1, Whitland's traffic fell off, unlike that at other places where there was an initial increase in ticket sales and freight carried before the drop into the Depression. At Whitland station the fall continued until 'rock bottom' was reached in 1930 — and even then 23,000 tickets were sold and the sum of £31,000 was earned. Afterwards, trade took off in leaps and bounds up to the advent of World War 2 when the old traffic in bombs and ambulance trains returned. Some details follow:

| | Staff | Paybill £ | Income £ | Tickets | General merchandise | | Cattle fwd |
					Fwd (tons)	Rec (tons)	
1923	48	8,420	24,852	38,716 (56)	3,102	4,897	625
1929	47	7,326	22,589	29,457 (27)	1,027	4,086	690
1930	46	7,557	21,639	29,024 (14)	1,709	5,085	684
1933	45	6,731	31,730	23,213 (15)	1,233	4,320	497
1938	43	7,371	76,292	20,417	736	409	318

The 1930s saw the typical decrease in train services, but of course the war changed that and the postwar boom of the 1950s maintained the number of trains at levels far above those that applied in the so-called 'Golden Age' of the GWR during the Edwardian period. In 1955 there were at least 88 daily scheduled main line trains at Whitland, against 54 in 1908. The increase was in all types of train — notably in the number of long-distance 'A' class expresses and the extra fish, parcels and meat trains. The famous and ancient 3.50pm Milford Haven to Paddington 'Trawl Fish', one of the GWR's fastest and heaviest goods trains, was still running and extra milk trains from

Whitland to Wood Lane, such as the 3.50pm and 5.25pm 'Whitland Milk' had become well established by 1955. Compared to 1936 (there were no milk trains as such from Whitland in 1908) there were two extra milk trains, three extra fish trains and three extra parcels trains in 1955. The branch lines were running as busily as ever and it must have been good to be alive on Whitland station in 1955. Even the Cardigan branch was running four goods trains instead of the two scheduled before the war! The following table shows what might have been seen at Whitland by the signalman if everything was running to time.

Lunchtime trains at Whitland — weekdays 1955

Train	11.10 M H'v'n	1.10 OOC	11.20 P Dock	12.00 M H'v'n	12.52 N'berth	6.35 T't'n	9.12 C'diff	10.40 P Dock
Class	A	D	K	A	K	B	C	K
Arr	11.58	11.58	12.40	12.52	1.09	1.27	1.50 Parcels	2.00
Dep	12.04 To Padd	12.10 To F'g'd		12.57 To Padd		1.32 To N'land	2.10 To N'land	

M H'v'n	Milford Haven	N'berth	Narberth
OOC	Old Oak Common	T't'n	Taunton
P Dock	Pembroke Dock	C'diff	Cardiff
N'land	Neyland	F'g'd	Fishguard

The 'crack' train at Whitland between 1953 and 1962 was the 10.55am Paddington and the opposite working which for most of its life left Pembroke at around 1pm — the exact time varied slightly over the years. This was the up and the down 'Pembroke Coast Express', calling all stations between Pembroke and Whitland, but otherwise an 'A' headcode train and one of the very fastest on Western Region. 'Manor'-hauled through Whitland, it usually had a fine GWR green engine with fancy headboard and smart brown and cream coaches — a real morale-booster of a train. It continued to run for a while after dieselisation but without any of the special feeling that it had under steam. The Cardigan branch closed, steam operated to the last by '16xx' 0-6-0PTs and '45xx' 2-6-2Ts on 10 September 1962, when dieselisation was in full swing. A daily goods service was retained for another eight months. Whitland shed closed to steam on 9 September 1963 and was closed completely in January 1966. Whitland today remains as the junction for Pembroke. It is now a windswept, bleak sort of place but at least it is still in use.

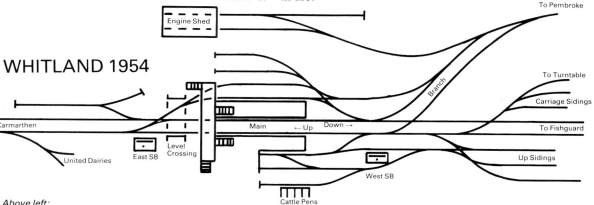

WHITLAND 1954

Above left:
The view west from the footbridge as '61XX' 2-6-2T No 6116 arrives with a train from Pembroke in the summer of 1961. The site of the old P&TR station is in left middle distance.
John Stimpson/Author's Collection

Below:
A look east along the up platform in 1961 showing the crossing gates and a glimpse of the East signalbox.
Lens of Sutton

Yeovil

Above:
The exterior of Pen Mill station about 110 years after it was opened. *Reg Farrell/Author's Collection*

The first rails into Yeovil were laid by the independent Bristol & Exeter Railway (B&ER) as a broad gauge, single track from Durston Junction on their main line a few miles east of Taunton. The branch came southeast through Langport to a terminus called Hendford about a mile west of Yeovil town centre. The line was opened to passenger traffic on 1 October 1853 and to goods on 26th of that month. The next railway to arrive was the GWR with their broad gauge, single track Wilts, Somerset & Weymouth line which was opened to a station called Pen Mill, just over one mile east of the town centre on 1 September 1856. On 20 January 1857 the route was opened through to Weymouth.

Pen Mill station became a junction on 2 February when the B&ER opened a 1½-mile link line connecting the two railways around the south side of the town and in so doing put their terminus on a spur. The London & South Western Railway was at this time driving a railway westwards from Salisbury to Exeter and using a local company — the Salisbury & Yeovil Railway (S&YR), which was leased to the LSWR as soon as it was complete — the LSWR brought a standard gauge, single track to Hendford. The S&YR crossed the GWR on a bridge 1⅜ track miles south of Pen Mill and ran alongside the GWR for a few hundred yards before turning west alongside the B&ER link line to Hendford Junction. Here, the track was mixed gauge to allow LSWR trains to reverse into and

out of the B&ER terminus, the LSWR passenger service from Salisbury commencing on 1 June 1860. This formed a new 'break of gauge' and all goods traffic had to be transshipped by hand between the two lines.

On 19 July 1860 the LSWR opened its route to Exeter which served a station called Yeovil Junction about two track miles south of Pen Mill. A Salisbury-facing junction was formed ⅝-mile east of the new station to allow trains to run to Hendford direct from Salisbury, but this was soon abandoned and a shuttle service was instituted between Yeovil Junction and the Hendford terminus.

Hendford, built for one company's trains, was sadly overcrowded by those of three, and in particular both by the constant need for trains to reverse in and out and the need to transfer all freight between broad and narrow gauge wagons. To improve matters, a handsome Joint station was built about a mile east of Hendford called Yeovil Town. This was opened on 1 June 1861 and the line from Yeovil Junction to it was doubled at the same time. Yeovil Town station had a double set of staff (B&ER and LSWR), and two booking offices. The easternmost office in the building was

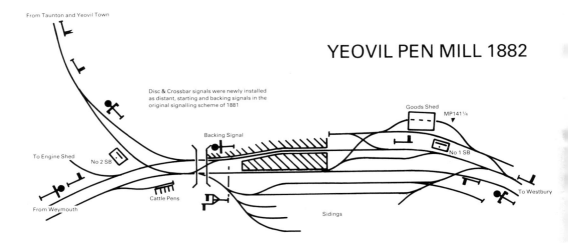

YEOVIL PEN MILL 1882

From Taunton and Yeovil Town

Disc & Crossbar signals were newly installed as distant, starting and backing signals in the original signalling scheme of 1881

Goods Shed

MP141¼

Backing Signal

No 1 SB

To Engine Shed

No 2 SB

To Westbury

From Weymouth

Cattle Pens

Sidings

the LSWR's, the engine shed was jointly owned and complicated indeed were the arrangements covering which company paid for what and how much. Issues such as what portion of the rent from the refreshment rooms should go to each party led to years of long arguments.

While the passenger arrangements were now easy, the congestion at Hendford for freight was as bad as ever. To extricate itself from the mess the GWR built a new transfer point right alongside the down main line at Yeovil Junction. This was the 36-chain Clifton May Bank branch opened on 13 June 1864. The line forked right about 1¼ miles south of Pen Mill, passed through the LSWR embankment on a 1 in 85 gradient and shortly reached a level with LSWR tracks. Broad gauge tracks passed on each side of an island platform and one continued into a transfer shed where a siding from the LSWR arrived. After the GWR converted the Weymouth line to the standard gauge on 22 June 1874 it was possible for whole trains to be transferred through the sidings at Clifton May Bank and at some stage the necessary connection was made.

From 1 January 1876 the B&ER became part of the GWR and the Town station became a Joint GWR/LSWR undertaking. The GWR had a shed at Pen Mill so the LSWR took over the Town shed entirely and paid the GWR £80 a year for the privilege.

On 23 February 1881 the GWR and LSWR jointly agreed that the Town station should be 'locked' — that is, equipped with modern signalling. This was done at an estimated cost of £1,536 shared equally between the two companies, and from 30 March 1882 Yeovil Town station was controlled by two signalboxes. The signalmen were employed as Joint staff and were paid in alternate years by the GWR and LSWR. These men's duties

were 'to work the signalboxes on day and night duty alternately, to attend to the ground points and to guard the premises'. This reads as if they were still regarded as policemen rather than signalmen. The Pen Mill station was also worked through two 'locking boxes'. No 1 locking box, which later became North box, had 24 levers of which 17 were in use, No 2 box, which later became South box, was situated in the 'V' of the junction and had 21 levers of which 18 were in use. Both these boxes were in use by 24 October 1881. Clifton May Bank signalbox was in existence in 1884 and was replaced in 1896 by a 21-lever box standing in the 'V' of the junction. The branch was worked with a wooden train staff throughout its life. In 1904 and 1910 there were two exchange trips a day, one each morning and evening. In 1929 there were three and so useful was the branch that it survived the 1929-33 economy drive and only succumbed on 7 June 1937, still carrying three trips a day. The signalbox was abolished on 1 November of that year. Yeovil Town's two signalboxes — East and West — survived until 1916 when they were replaced by one, GWR, brick box with a hip gabled roof. This had 41 working levers and stood at the west end of the station between the GWR single line to Durston and the LSWR double track connection to the Waterloo to Exeter main line. Of course, the single track was officially the 'main line' here and the South Western the 'branch'.

Pen Mill had a curious arrangement of tracks whereby a single track, the up main, snaked between two platforms under a Brunellian overall roof while the down main, following a smooth curve, came alongside one platform face with only the usual canopy to protect passengers from the elements. Pen Mill's roofed station was an 'up market' version of those provided at Frome and Warminster but looking more like that at

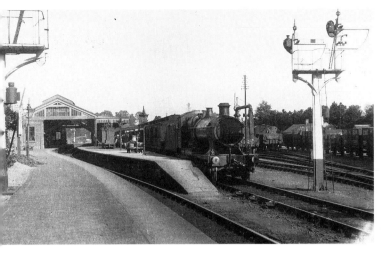

Left:
The view north along the up platform about 1925. A 'Bulldog'-hauled express train is signalled away for Weymouth as passengers and staff jostle around the open carriage doors. Note the old style wooden bracket signals. The nearest one has two subsidiary arms mounted low down the post and their lamp cases can be seen. *Lens of Sutton*

Below left:
A few years later and the bracket signal on the platform has been replaced by a straight post with a single arm and a route-indicating stencil below. The sidings give the air of a prosperous station with freight wagons, milk vans and spare carriages standing around. In the far distance the old North box can be seen. *Author's Collection*

Below:
Looking south through the station before World War 1. *Lens of Sutton*

Left:
The 1937 vintage signalbox at Pen Mill station on 2 March 1974.
Author

controlled by a 33-lever signalbox called Yeovil
South Junction which was built to the wartime
ARP (Air Raid Precautions) design. The junction
was for ambulance and other government trains
and, until 1966 was not normally used for
passenger trains or civilian freight. Once the war
was over the box remained switched out for
months or even years at a stretch.

The GWR engine shed at Pen Mill was a
wooden, broad gauge railway construction looking
very much like the one erected in the 1850s at
Oxford. It stood on a narrow, curved strip of land
between the river Yeo and the Town branch and
remained in use for 102 years. In 1922 it had an
allocation of nine engines including 5ft 2in 4-4-0
No 3552, '517' 0-4-2T No 3576 and 'Metro' 2-4-0T
No 626. There were also six powerful saddle tanks
for working local and longer distance freight and
for banking at Castle Cary and Yetminster. In
December 1947 the shed had 10 locomotives —
2-6-2Ts Nos 4572, 5529 and 5565 and 0-6-0PTs
Nos 3671, 3733, 4689, 5767, 9601, 9615 and 9771.
In addition to these the shed had six diesel railcars,
Nos 20, 21, 24, 28, 37 and 38. This dramatically
demonstrates the upsurge in traffic between 1922
and 1947.

The train service and income at Pen Mill stood
up well to the difficult years after World War 1 and
in particular from 1926. Indeed, a peak of ticket
sales was reached in that black year 1929 while
season ticket sales increased continuously. Some
details follow below.

Henley-on-Thames owing to the glass screens at
the gable ends. Everything at Pen Mill lasted a
long time. The engine shed, built in 1857, was
never replaced. The Brunellian roof was most
thoughtlessly pulled down by the GWR in the late
1920s or early 1930s and the North and South
signalboxes, which had once controlled disc and
crossbar signals, were not abolished until 14 February 1937 — well into the age of the diesel railcar.
They were replaced by a single, brick, hip roofed
signalbox, sited between the up and down main
lines at the north end of the station. This had 65
levers, of which 56 were working, but they
controlled a layout that had changed only
minimally since 1881. A new layout was created
1,000yd south of Pen Mill on 13 October 1943
when a double track junction from the GWR down
main to the SR up branch and from the SR down
branch to the GWR up main was opened. This was

Passenger Receipts

	Staff	Paybill £	Income £	Tickets	Income multiple of paybill
1903	47	3,393	19,519	96,785 (40)	5.75
1923	41	6,821	18,751	59,703 (40)	2.74
1929	39	6,452	24,404	64,955 (16)	3.78
1930	40	6,550	23,560	59,421 (28)	3.54
1933	39	6,565	19,365	58,093 (410)	2.94
1938	36	6,620	21,634	59,155 (865)	3.26

Goods traffic was handled as a separate department to the passenger side. Some details are
provided below.

	Staff	Paybill £	Income £	Minerals fwd (tons)	General merchandise Fwd (tons)	General merchandise Rec (tons)	Cattle fwd
1913	23	1,633	27,364	906	7,055	25,121	1,109
1923	32	5,311	63,505	2,328	7,979	25,877	976
1929	41	7,669	87,546	8,016	9,990	28,146	1,051
1930	45	8,085	80,712	7,390	10,497	18,411	1,190
1933	40	6,801	56,406	2,026	5,958	7,975	710
1938	42	8,074	63,590	2,263	6,489	12,701	453

In 1913, income from goods traffic was 16.75 times greater than the wages paid to goods department staff, but by 1938 tonnages sent away from Pen Mill were down and income was only 7.87 times greater than wages.

After World War 2 the number of trains running was higher than at any time in the railway's history, 1914-18 excepted. In 1954 the 1934 service was still running but with many extra trains. Passenger trains tended to start earlier in the morning showing up a social trend for working far away from home each day. Main line goods trains no longer carried the brunt of pick-up traffic at Pen Mill but instead a system of long-distance pick-up goods, radiating from Yeovil as their centre, serviced the local stations and took the wagons to Westbury or Taunton yards. Thus Yeovil's freight traffic took longer to get where it was going.

The loss of the three round trips to Clifton May Bank was more than balanced by the seven transfer trips which ran each day between Pen Mill, Town and Hendford Goods depot. Shunting

Above:
The 12.30pm Paddington to Weymouth express, 'Castle' hauled, pulls away from Pen Mill with the engine shed to the right and the cattle pens on the left. The building at the far end of the pens was the ground frame hut housing the levers working the points to the siding and the Annett's key instrument by which the lever was released. The Pen Mill signalman pulled his lever 20 to release the Annett's key. The Yeovil Town branch is on the right. 16 July 1958. *R. C. Riley*

Below right:
The Pen Mill station pilot, 2-6-2T No 5542, waits on the down main line for the crossover to the up main to be reversed. Above the roof of the ground frame are a pair of banner repeater signals arranged to repeat the indication of the junction signals ahead at Yeovil South Junction. 10 July 1956. *R. C. Riley*

power was much in demand at Yeovil in 1954-55 and the shed was still supplying six pilot engines as it had done 30 years before. Pilots Nos 1, 2 and 3 were for Pen Mill and Hendford with 4hr shunting booked to them each day. The fourth engine ran 'light' to Castle Cary to shunt that yard and act as banker while the sixth engine acted as the Pen Mill pilot and Yetminster/Evershot banker as required.

Although there were more passenger trains running in 1955 than 1935, these in 1955 were

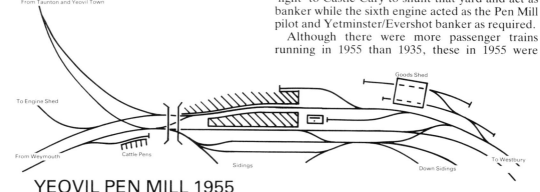

YEOVIL PEN MILL 1955

much slower. Since the early 1920s there had been four 'crack' trains at Pen Mill, the 12.30pm and 6.00pm Paddington to Weymouth expresses, the 3.40pm (sometimes 3.50pm) Weymouth Quay and the 4.10pm Weymouth Town to Paddington expresses — the 3.40pm being the Channel Islands Boat Train. Both of these called at Pen Mill and in 1929, 1936 and 1955 they always made the same connection to Taunton. In 1929 and 1936, passengers off the boat train had nearly an hour to wait but in 1955 the wait was shorter because their train took longer to reach Pen Mill. However, the pattern was identical. The 12.30pm Paddington called at six stations on the journey to Pen Mill in 1929, 1936 and 1955 and lost 21min in station time in the process. In 1929 the overall time from Paddington to Pen Mill, a distance of 127 miles, was 171min but in 1955 the train took 13min longer. In 1955 the Town station still had the 'Joint' atmosphere as GWR engines continued to work goods and passenger trains to and from Hendford or Taunton, passing on their way Bulleid Pacifics, 'King Arthur' 4-6-0s and 'M7' 0-4-4Ts to name but a few of the Southern engines present on the shed and at the Town station. There were 13 trips each way for the Southern push-pull train shuttling between the Town and Junction stations, lots of light engine movements and several main line expresses and stopping trains between Waterloo and Salisbury, Exeter and Ilfracombe and Yeovil Town station. The first time the author saw Yeovil was from the window of a shuttle in 1959. The sight of that sylvan glen south of Pen Mill, filled with a four track railway line, large double junction and plenty of signals fairly took his breath away. The table below gives a summary of trains through Pen Mill in one hour on a weekday morning in 1955.

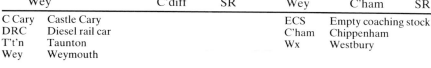

	7.26	From	6.45		5.45	7.17	6.25	7.30
	C Cary	T't'n	Wey		B'tol	Wey	Wx	Wx
	DRC		ECS				Loco Coal	Milk MT
	B	B	C	G	B	B	H	C
Arr	7.50 n/s	7.57			8.16	8.33	8.35	8.50
Dep	7.55		8.10	8.15	8.22	8.38	8.50	9.05
	To Wey		To C'diff	To SR	To Wey	To C'ham	To SR	To Wey

C Cary	Castle Cary	ECS	Empty coaching stock
DRC	Diesel rail car	C'ham	Chippenham
T't'n	Taunton	Wx	Westbury
Wey	Weymouth		

The first route lost to Yeovil was that to Taunton, closed on 6 July 1964. The Town station remained open and the Yeovil Junction shuttle ran to Pen Mill via the Town until 3 October 1966 when someone remembered Yeovil South Junction box and, for the first time in its life, it was opened on a regular basis to permit the shuttle to run direct to Pen Mill and to allow the closure of Town station. This was too good to last and the service was abolished on 6 May 1968 along with the goods service from Pen Mill to Hendford, the latter place then becoming a parcels depot without rail access. The double track main line south of Pen Mill was converted into two parallel single tracks on 26 May 1968. Trains for Weymouth or Yeovil Junction could be put on the correct track at Pen Mill and Yeovil South Junction box was abolished. By that time the only trains for the Junction were permanent way wagons, the rare diverted passenger train and a single, scheduled freight from Salisbury to Exeter via Westbury and Yeovil Pen Mill which took that route so that Westbury drivers could maintain their knowledge of the connecting link line. Now even this has gone, but at least Pen Mill station, with its odd platform system is still open for business.

Above:
The same location as the previous photograph, 37 years later, but still offering a wonderful selection of Southern motive power. The Joint station building can be seen clearly here and in particular the tower-like blocks at each end, designed to give each company separate office accommodation. The LSWR offices were in the nearest end of the building. 17 August 1963.
B. J. Ashworth

Right:
Waiting to shuttle back to Yeovil Junction, ex-LBSCR 'D1' Class 0-4-2T No 2273 rests in Yeovil Town station with two auto-coaches and a gas tank. The view looks towards Hendford with a Drummond 'Black Motor' 0-6-0 in the distance. All the signals are GWR in accordance with the long standing Joint agreement. 21 May 1935. *H. C. Casserley*

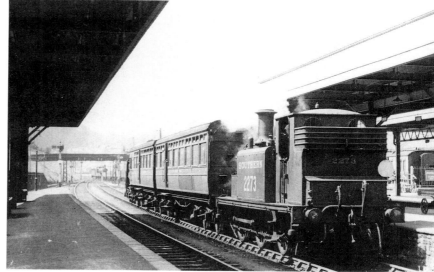

Bottom right:
The 1916 vintage GWR signalbox at Yeovil Town minus its cast iron name plate and carrying a Southern Region green and white enamel board. The view looks towards Pen Mill and the gable end of the Joint station. In the foreground is the double track line from Yeovil Junction which merges into Hendford siding behind the camera. One Southern Railway signal has arrived to break with tradition. 8 February 1963. *British Rail*

Additional information

Forepiece	Kinghams	p 70
Title page	Yeovil Town	p 111
Contents page	Castle Cary	p 10
End piece	Castle Cary	p 13
Rear cover – top	Yeovil Pen Mill	p 106
Rear cover – bottom	Wellington (Salop)	p 93